the TOTAL PACKAGE

OWN Your Profitable Personal Brand

———

JuliAnn Stitick

The The Total Package: OWN Your Profitable Personal Brand

by JuliAnn Stitick
Cover Design by Becky Rickett
Copyright © 2015 by JuliAnn Stitick

ISBN: 978-1-944177-10-2 (e)
ISBN: 978-1-944177-11-9 (p)

Crescendo Publishing, LLC
300 Carlsbad Village Drive
Ste. 108A, #443
Carlsbad, California 92008-2999

www.CrescendoPublishing.com
GetPublished@CrescendoPublishing.com

A Message from the Author

Visit the VIDEO LINK below to hear a personal message from JuliAnn.

http://www.TheTotalPackageBook.com

RESOURCES, TOOLS AND GIFTS!!

I am providing you with some great resources,
tools and gifts I know you'll love!

Get instant access to these at
http://www.TheTotalPackageBook.com/gifts

A Special Thanks

Writing a book has always been on my bucket list but the thought of it felt very daunting. Once I made the decision to step beyond my fear and take action, the first call I made was to my sister Janine asking for her support. We have always had very different personalities and took drastically different paths in our professional lives. She earned her Master's degree in education and taught English for over 20 years while I quit college and took the entrepreneurial route. This project has been a beautiful blend of our diverse talents, and it has been a most amazing experience.

Janine, thank you for bringing your brilliance to the table by creating structure and flow to my words while allowing my true voice to be heard. I love you.

Table of Contents

Chapter One
First Impressions

-1-

First Impressions

The beautiful white marble floor of the luxury hotel bathroom shined up at me as I finished up in the restroom stall. I could hear the sink running while two conference attendees were discussing the upcoming presentation I would give right after the lunch break. Obviously, they didn't know I was in the bathroom because one of the women said, "I'm not sure this Juli-Ann understands the issues 'real' women go through. I mean just look at her...she's skinny and blonde and gorgeous." My heart sank and of course, I felt a profound sense of sadness. However, I had a few responsibilities to take care of before the lunch break, so I didn't have the luxury of remaining in the stall until they left. As I walked up to the sink to wash, the women blanched, smiled nervously and quickly left the ladies' room.

After the salmon salad and lemon tart with coffee, it was time for me to hit the stage. I must say I felt a little insecure, knowing that I had already been dismissed based on my appearance and really wanted to make a connection with those women--a connection I knew would make an imprint on how they were seeing themselves. I took a couple of deep breaths for confidence and calm, took the stage and gave it my all.

Later with the PowerPoint turned off, my mic unclipped from my lapel and the applause fading in my ears, I headed out to the lobby to meet and greet at my display table. Those two women from the ladies' room made their way to the front of the line; they simultaneously hugged me and said, "We felt so bad that you heard us earlier. You really do GET us! We're so sorry for what we said."

They were not being mean and spiteful earlier in the restroom; they were just doing what we all do: making a judgment of someone based on an initial impression. I'm not saying it didn't hurt hearing it, but thankfully it came at an opportune time for me. It was a dramatic illustration. Their impression of me was their reality of me, but I had the chance to expand their perception.

The raw truth is that people do judge you based on their perception, and your personal branding is the lens through which you will be perceived, evaluated and eventually hired.

So let's get right to the point. *The Total Package: OWN Your Profitable Personal Brand* is a book, my lifetime in the making. For years, especially the last 20, I have dreamed that at some point I would put down in print the expertise I've gained from my experiences, both personally and professionally. At first, I wasn't ready because who would read a book written by someone with an incomplete college education (apparently my own judgment of myself) and no 'formal' training in my industry (YIKES)? Once I got over those hang-ups, I wavered about what the book should really be. Was it a memoir of my rocky journey--a journey that doesn't define me? Should it be a strategic 'how to' on style? Should I share my expertise on personal brand development?

One afternoon my business coach, Lisa said, "JuliAnn, it's time for the book."

My response was, "But I'm not really ready. I haven't figured out all of the pieces yet."

She reminded me of something I tell my clients all of the time, "It's not going to be perfect ever, but it will never happen if you don't just do it!!" Okay, Okay.

I'm a 'cut to the chase' kind of woman who doesn't like to waste time, so here we are. I've cherry picked the elements that are most critical to developing a successful personal brand—a brand that will attract, engage and monetize! The good news is that this book will not take you long to read, but it is packed with insightful, savvy tips, and, in the end, you'll begin to see yourself in a renewed light. Then you'll be a complete and total package.

5 Keys to a Profitable Personal Brand

The 5 Keys are Identity, Image, Language, Online Presence and Customer Experience. They are meant to be addressed in exactly that order as you build your brand persona. In other words, don't jump to online presence before you've had the opportunity to flesh out your identity or work on your image and language.

The Big Mistake

PLEASE READ CAREFULLY!! One of the biggest mistakes I see over and over is that professionals complete the branding process in the wrong sequence. Time after time, clients come to me after they've developed their logo, rushed to get business cards printed and launched a website. They have spent time and money on incomplete personal branding with a look and feel that is not them at their best. Then they decide to 'treat' themselves by hiring a personal branding expert. The issue is that once they develop their personal brand, they begin to see themselves in an entirely new light with more insight, clarity and confidence and then they say, "Ugh! I would have branded my business with a very different look--one that is me at my best!" S(he) is frustrated, and rightly so, that she has wasted precious resources developing a brand without branding her persona first. Is personal branding a luxury or treat? Neither! It is the crucial foundation upon which your business brand should be built.

This book is about the practice of marketing yourself as a brand with some of the same strategies as the big guns like Nike, Coca-Cola or Apple. A well-executed personal brand is strong, consistent and specific. It encompasses all of the fine details that address the first impression to the follow-up and beyond. Personal branding is common among celebrities, politicians and sports figures. Think of Shark Tank's Barbara Corcoran, or the jazz styling of Michael Buble´, and also Virgin mogul Richard Branson. Each has a reputation for their established and consistent personal brand, and they top it off with their signature look—a look in alignment with their branding, marketing, etc. and you better believe it's by design.

Successful entrepreneurs understand that developing a strong personal brand is even more important than their products and services because while those goods and services might be top notch, no one will know about them if the personal brand representing them doesn't capture the attention and curiosity of the prospective customer.

Your Total Package

Jenny and I were sitting in an elegant dressing room at Nordstrom. We were discussing our shopping strategies for the day. Timidly, she explained that she was a little uncomfortable about getting undressed. First I asked some gentle but probing questions about why she felt that way, and she went on to tell me that she wasn't feeling very good about her body, all 5'2', size 4/6 of her.

I explained that I have never worked with a client who didn't have some level of body image insecurity. Further, I told her that "the dressing room experience" is one of the most transformative pieces of my work. It's a space where I have the ability to unconditionally accept a woman, no matter how she feels about her body. As Jenny and I continued to talk, it struck me that it would be daunting for her to disrobe in front of me because, as usual, I was in my stylish business attire. The vulnerability was so crystal clear that I needed to do something drastic. So for the very first time in front of a client, I pulled one of my boots off, and then the other. I continued taking off my pants and top as well. I stood boldly in the center of the dressing room in only my bra and underwear.

As I spun around, I asked her to take a good look. "My butt is a little jiggly, and I just can't get my abs to firm up the way I want them too, but what defines me is not how I look. I am still a good person and a successful businesswoman even though I have cellulite. My tummy is bloated, but I'm a good person. I wish my legs were a little firmer and I didn't have muffin top, but I'm a good person. What matters most is the impact I make in the world." Jenny sat there with tears in her eyes and invited me to take part in her dressing room experience. She instinctively knew she could see herself through new eyes.

The next day, I received this heartfelt and powerful email;

Dear JuliAnn,

Good morning, Beautiful! I feel absolutely compelled and inspired to write you a note of gratitude to let you know how much I appreciate you.

First, thank you so much for yesterday. What an incredible experience that was. Way, way outside my comfort zone, but so incredibly worth it. You have forever shifted my perception about my personal brand and image.

Here are a few results I feel already:

- *More confidence in who I am and what I do*
- *An increased feeling of self-worth*
- *A deeper appreciation for myself and my time*
- *More pride in my appearance*
- *A desire to have more in my life - like suddenly the old way of being is no longer acceptable*
- *An increased feeling of generosity - for example, now that I have more, I can let go of some of the old stuff and one of the first thoughts I had was I'm not going to hoard old stuff in my closet that I now know doesn't work for me - I've donated it to someone who needs it more than I do*
- *More excitement about living a higher quality of life*

I am forever changed after that transformative experience.

And with regards to you and the experience of working with you - what you did for me in the dressing room was the most incredible display of commitment and customer service that I could ever imagine. You are an absolute artist and creative genius when it comes to the craft of your work. You are intuitive and have an innate ability to sense how I felt and what I liked and didn't like, to come up with the perfect outfits.

I was also so impressed with the way you took care of me as a client during the day - thank you for pampering me. It's really nice to be taken care of and to remember how good that feels, so thank you for reminding me. I want you to know that it made a really big difference to me.

I can't say thank you enough. You are really a gift. And you are so very talented! It was truly a privilege to spend the day with you. I already knew you were fabulous before, but having the experience of working with you in that way elevated my understanding and appreciation for you and what you do, and took it to the next level.

And on a professional level - since I now know exactly what you do I could not be more excited to share you with others. I am beyond excited to send business your way. And the service you provide is so far beyond what you charge for your services. (How can you even put a price tag on the results I listed above?) I am excited to communicate that to others.

And one last thing - as a role model - you are the most beautiful example of who I aspire to be. Thank you for that. It's so much more than just how you look and how your carry yourself - it's the fact that you are this beautiful, classy and elegant woman who lights up the room, commands the respect of others and comes across as someone who is and should be well taken care of by others, but at the same time you have the humility and the heart of a person who is truly of service to others - to be able to really take care of someone else and treat them like they are just as valuable as you are. I don't think I've ever seen that modeled before by anyone. It's important to have the personal experience of being around people who inspire you and show you what to aspire to - and you have definitely done that for me.

What more can I say beyond thank you and I love you and completely adore you :)

Jenny

It is not coincidental that I received this message just as I sat down to write the introduction of The Total Package. The beauty of her words was a confirmation that I am walking my walk and not just teaching others to walk it. My brand experience exemplifies that my values are expressed throughout my personal brand identity.

Jenny had a shift in her own perception and image even before she donned her new duds for others to see. She now knows her true transformation wasn't just her outward appearance. She can see the beauty and possibilities within herself. She now has more clarity and an elevated mindset in the language she will use whether non-verbal, written or spoken.

She's excited for her upcoming photo shoot, new branding and online presence because she now has complete clarity about who she is at her ultimate potential, and she has the confidence to show it! Finally, realizing 'suddenly the old way of being is no longer acceptable,' Jenny will model that in working with her clients. No doubt that will transform the customer experience her clients have.

There are five key elements to developing a personal brand people will love. In this book I'll unpack each item with real-world examples* which will help you apply the elements in your own unique way. As someone born with an entrepreneurial spirit, my mindset has always been to jump into action and figure it out along the way. Yes, I've made many mistakes, but I've learned valuable, applicable lessons from each one. So this book is my gift to you. You can learn from my experience and develop your Total Package in a strategic and profitable way.

*In my client examples, the names have been changed.

Chapter Two
Key One: Identity

-2-

Key One: Identity

"Hide not your talents. They for use were made.
What's a sundial in the shade?"
Benjamin Franklin

I was raised in a textbook Southern California middle-class home, but still I grew up with a sense of needing to hide. My loving, hardworking, committed father owned a wheel alignment business and my warm, dedicated mom worked with my father, volunteered in the PTA, and had a hot homemade dinner on the table at 6:00 pm sharp every night, except for the nights we treated ourselves to Taco Bell, Billy's Deli or Bob's Big Boy. Most Sundays we attended church, then went to brunch at Du-Par's, and later watched Mutual of Omaha's Wild Kingdom followed by The Wonderful World of Disney while we ate popcorn and sipped root beer floats for dinner! School came fairly easy to me as did making friends of all kinds. I usually had a big smile on my face and was able to bring the sunshine into a room...or a thunder cloud.

If you looked at me from the outside, you would have thought I had it all, and I did- for the most part. What you wouldn't have seen was the fact that I kept the shameful secret of sexual abuse to myself. It happened at such a young age that I was genuinely unaware of anything different and so I didn't even think to tell my parents. I became keenly adept at hiding who I was on the inside by 'looking perfect' on the outside so others would not know the shameful truth of who I perceived myself to be. I became fascinated by all things hair, makeup, and wardrobe. I knew how to look the part of having it all together which covered the suffering on the inside. As I entered adolescence, it became more and more difficult to stuff the feelings of inadequacy and pain, so I turned to drugs and alcohol for relief. It worked for a while.

As I grew into adulthood, married and had children, I realized that the poor choices I was making were hurting more than just me. They were hurting my husband and children, and I wasn't willing to continue living that way. So I reached out for the spiritual guidance, professional services and group support I needed to begin the healing process and get healthy… mentally, emotionally, physically and spiritually.

I wanted to be known, heard and feel like I mattered. Isn't that what we all want deep down inside?

During this time, my professional life was picking up. Without really knowing it at the time, my mission and passion were to help others love themselves and reflect that to the world. All marketing language aside, I never actually realized the benefits I was delivering. I never knew that by championing and advocating for them, I was healing myself as well.

So here I am, someone who wanted to be known from a heart space… very successfully teaching others how to make themselves known. Oh, the irony of it. There were times I even questioned my 'credentials' because I felt like a complete and utter fraud. Who was I to be teaching something I struggled with myself? What I now know is that is exactly why I'm so effective in my craft and why my clients know that I care for them personally as well as their professional success.

What does that have to do with YOUR personal brand identity? It has everything to do with it.

What Defines You?

The first step in developing your personal brand identity is to clearly define who you are. Once you understand who you are as an individual, then the brand will flow from there. Of course, you have your own personal journey and you are dynamic and changing, but there are fundamental truths about who you are, what matters to you and of course... what you love. It is crucial that you be as authentic as possible. You brand your persona because YOU are the common thread that can create a consistent and cohesive brand identity--one that is as unique and compelling as you are.

Defining who you are allows you to lead naturally from your experiences and strengths. I am an artist. I am an outgoing introvert. I am passionate and heart-centered. I love dogs, country music and reading. I am also open-hearted, compassionate, playful and have a childlike curiosity. These 'definitions' are woven throughout my personal brand identity, the particular language I use in marketing and creating content for my social media posts, and the personal examples I share from the stage.

As a big movie fan, I never miss awards season--The Oscars, Golden Globes, etc. Without fail, when George Clooney takes the stage the reception is one of smiles, generous applause and a real sense of love from his colleagues. His interactions are warm, authentic, and full of laughter. He stands out as classy, friendly, approachable, self-deprecating and a team player, and that's exactly what makes him compelling, too.

Others are attracted to him for those very reasons--not to mention his good looks and style (I would have been remiss not to mention that!). From Clooney's humble Kentucky upbringing where he worked as a shoe salesman and a tobacco farmhand before his rise to fame, it is his family's values and strong work ethic that have served him so well. Clooney is an actor, icon, activist, and humanitarian. Although a man in the spotlight, George Clooney seems to have the ability to protect most of his personal life from the public. This adds to his mystique-- another asset of his personal brand. It's also in alignment with his sense of humility. Clooney stands for supporting others, whether it's his philanthropic efforts in Darfur or his passion for spotlighting other artists, ushering them forward in their careers. This work enables fans and peers to connect with him in a meaningful way. He provides no reason for people not to like him. There are few superstars or icons who can match this aspect of Clooney's persona.

Defining who you are can be a challenge because you can't see the label from inside the bottle. Also, many of us spend more of our time fixing what's wrong with us rather than developing what's right. Chances are you may not know the depth of your strengths. That's why all of my personal clients begin their process with exercises and assessments.

Begin to think broadly about your personality and how others experience you. Do others call you 'the plan maker'? That might mean you have great leadership and organizational skills. Do people like being around you because you make them laugh? That might mean you inspire others to see the bright side of life.

Your client testimonials are a treasure trove for defining your brand identity. After all, the words of praise are from your ideal clients- those that have chosen to hire you already. What speaks to them about your brand experience will no doubt speak to others, too. Take note of their key language or phrasing and repurpose that into your brand.

If you're short on customer testimonials, it's time to ask for them. You can request them from existing clients by letting them know you would like to include theirs on your website. Be sure to ask them specifically how they'd like to be identified and let them know you'll include a link to their website. If you're asked how long their quote should be, give them the leeway to write as little or much as they'd like. Then you can pull out the key phrases you know will speak to your potential clients.

When a customer expresses happiness with my services, I immediately ask more pointed questions and then ask permission to quote them. Here are some examples:

Joan: "JuliAnn, I'm so happy I worked with you."

JuliAnn: "What specifically are you happy about?"

Joan: "I look and feel great. I have a renewed sense of myself and my confidence has increased."

JuliAnn: "I'm thrilled you are feeling that way. Joan, may I use your words as a testimonial?"

Joan: "Absolutely!"

Susan: "JuliAnn, I am being perceived on a higher level now."

JuliAnn: "How is that benefitting your work?"

Susan: "Now, I'm attracting the clients who value and can afford my services."

JuliAnn: "I love hearing that! May I quote you?"

Susan: "Please do."

Two independent assessments I suggest my clients take are: The Fascination Advantage Assessment by Sally Hogshead, author of #1 bestseller How the World Sees You. This assessment identifies your archetype and how others perceive you at your best.

The second evaluation that will help you define yourself at your best is Gallup's Strengths Finder 2.0 assessment. The Strengths Finder 2.0 assessment is a revised version of the 1998 assessment developed by the father of strengths psychology, Donald O. Clifton, Ph.D. and his associate Tom Rath. I love their philosophy of focusing on what people excel at rather than what needs fixing.

You can access your own Fascination Advantage Assessment and Strengths Finder 2.0 Assessment on links through my website: http://www.TheTotalPackageBook.com/gifts

A basic marketing principal is to identify your very narrow target market, connect with them, and the rest will follow. Once I began to strategically weave my own brand identity into my brand presence and marketing strategies, my target market started to appear and my visibility and bottom line accelerated substantially.

The value of 'defining who you are' is apparent in my client Rebecca's brand. She is a marketing consultant who develops strategies which her team then implements for her clients. However, if you had seen Rebecca's website, you would have thought she was executing everything herself which muddled the representation of who she is and what she stands for. Based on our Identity work, Rebecca clarified her role in her company as the leader and strategist. Taking that to her website, she presented herself as the leader of a strong support team involved in the implementation of those marketing approaches. She changed nothing within her company, but rather simply revealed her true role as the strategist. Once we clarified her strengths and role throughout her brand persona, she quickly began attracting the clients she had always dreamed of.

What Do You Value?

Every single one of us lives according to our highest values. Try as we might, we will never escape our values, many of which are instilled in us during our formative years. Your values define you in an even deeper way as they are the most important things in your life. Consider the people, experiences and emotions that fulfill and drive you the most, and you will find your values there. Discerning your values helps you tap into a more heightened and authentic personal brand.

My client Linda loves all animals and highly values the kind and loving treatment of them. This value is the cornerstone of her vegan health coach practice. She is incredibly effective at portraying her passion because it's a truth to her value system. Her values are clear throughout her brand as well. The philanthropic organizations she supports align with her values, her best-selling book highlights her heart for animals, and she regularly features her pets in her social media content and live presentations.

What are some of your highest values? Take some time to review the following list. There will be many that will resonate with you but try to narrow it down to a maximum of ten. That way you can focus your branding choices and marketing language around those that matter the most.

What Are Your Values?

Accountability	Economy
Accuracy	Effectiveness
Achievement	Efficiency
Adventurousness	Elegance
Altruism	Empathy
Ambition	Enjoyment
Assertiveness	Enthusiasm
Balance	Equality
Belonging	Excellence
Boldness	Excitement
Calmness	Expertise
Carefulness	Exploration
Commitment	Expressiveness
Community	Fairness
Compassion	Faith
Competitiveness	Fidelity
Consistency	Fitness
Contentment	Fluency
Contribution	Focus
Control	Freedom
Cooperation	Fun
Correctness	Generosity
Courtesy	Goodness
Creativity	Grace
Curiosity	Growth
Decisiveness	Happiness
Dependability	Hard Work
Determination	Health
Devoutness	Helping Society
Diligence	Holiness
Discipline	Honesty
Discretion	Honor
Diversity	Humility
Dynamism	

What Are Your Values?

Independence	Self-actualization
Ingenuity	Self-control
Inner Harmony	Selflessness
Inquisitiveness	Self-reliance
Insightfulness	Sensitivity
Intelligence	Serenity
Intellectual Status	Service
Intuition	Shrewdness
Joy	Simplicity
Justice	Soundness
Leadership	Speed
Legacy	Spontaneity
Love	Stability
Loyalty	Strategic
Making A Difference	Strength
Mastery	Structure
Merit	Success
Obedience	Support
Openness	Teamwork
Order	Temperance
Originality	Thankfulness
Patriotism	Thoroughness
Perfection	Thoughtfulness
Piety	Timeliness
Positivity	Tolerance
Practicality	Traditionalism
Preparedness	Trustworthiness
Professionalism	Truth-seeking
Prudence	Understanding
Quality-orientation	Uniqueness
Reliability	Usefulness
Resourcefulness	Vision
Restraint	Vitality
Security	

Now that you've identified your key values, it's time to weave them throughout your personal brand identity. My original value statement was "Aligning your personal brand and image with the level of success you desire." This statement highlighted my values of consistency, self-actualization, and success. However, the more I worked with my clients since creating that statement, the more I have become aware that this declaration didn't highlight self-actualization enough— a value I consistently strive for, and is most important to my work with clients. I changed the statement to, "Aligning your personal brand and image with your ultimate potential." Now it's in alignment with what I value most for my clients—seeing them develop their brand in accordance with their ultimate potential.

Ask For Feedback

You may want even more clarity about how others experience you. Firsthand, feedback is a valuable tool to craft your personal brand. Of course, you want to seek guidance from trusted professionals, but you can also reach out to others for their take on what you represent. They will see things that you don't and can help you eliminate your blind spots.

Here's an exercise I give my clients. It's called 5 & 5. Think of five individuals - business colleagues, clients, or simply acquaintances - people who are able to be objective. That way you'll get a clear picture of how you're perceived. Ask them to describe you using five adjectives. Some examples might be: smart, professional, funny, engaging, down-to-earth, or in-the-know, passionate, strategic, welcoming, enlightened. Get the idea? There's usually a common thread or two, so when the same (or similar) descriptors repeat themselves, it's important to take note.

Send a simple email like the one below to your trusted sources. Then be sure to print the results and post them so you can be reminded of the exceptional and accomplished person you are! In addition weave them throughout your brand identity.

Dear Friend/Colleague,

I'm reading JuliAnn Stitick's book The Total Package and am hoping to get some feedback on how you experience me as a person. Will you do a quick brainstorm and come up with five words that best describe me?

Here are some examples JuliAnn gave:

warm, funny, smart, successful, advocate
kind, spirited, savvy, heart-centered, philanthropist

edgy, powerful, attractive, sharp, motivated

Your input is valuable to me. Thanks so much for your time and insight.

Sincerely,

You

When Gina completed this exercise, she was pleasantly surprised to know that her five sources see her as a leader and innovator in her field of expertise. This feedback allowed Gina to confidently weave those descriptors throughout her brand presence in images, marketing language and choice of content. But even more importantly, her own confidence factor multiplied!

Be Bold and Authentically You

I feel a sense of sisterhood with any self-made woman, and Barbara Corcoran definitely fits that bill. Her spunky, colorful, smart, bold and straightforward approach has served her well. The first I had heard of Corcoran was from my hubby Joe when he came home from a conference at which he'd heard her speak. He told me she was someone I'd love, and he was right. Most people know her as a television personality--a "Shark" investor on ABC's Shark Tank. However, as always there's more. She is a wife, mother, businesswoman, investor, speaker, consultant, and author. Whew!

When I first clicked on her site www.BarbaraCorcoran.com, I was greeted with a cheerful, colorful, simple, elegant site. Her message was clear and her personal brand (or image) reflected a fun, sharp, warm woman. There were two things that really stood out for me, and I have since applied them in my own business as well as those of my clients. These two principals have resulted in oodles of success.

First, is Barbara's 'say it like it is' attitude which is evident on the 'About' page of her website. The first sentence highlights her terrible grades in school and her inability to find a job that was right for her. When you read further, you'll see how she was able to turn that around and become one of the most successful women in the world.

Another example of her spunky, straightforward approach is the title of one of her books If You Don't Have Big Breasts, Put Ribbons on Your Pigtails- and other lessons I learned from my Mom. Barbara is not afraid to be who she is and people LOVE her for it.

I use to temper who I was based on my audience, and while it can be argued that elements of that are strategic, I now show up as JuliAnn--a woman who is far from perfect, but invested in others looking and feeling their best and achieving great success in doing so! How can you elevate your 'say it like it is' attitude?

Barbara Corcoran is also very bold! She's not afraid to take risks and was willing to 'fake it' until she inadvertently built a very successful brand. Don't misunderstand me here. There was no wrongdoing on her part. She was willing to take action based on the belief of what was possible until it actually happened.

A year ago I was inspired to begin making very bold requests. A well-known business coach offered me a spot to speak at his event, but it would cost me $15,000. While that business model is common in some circles, it didn't work for me. He went on to say that he'd offer me an opportunity based on sharing the profits from my product sales that day. That still didn't work. His response was, "JuliAnn, this needs to be a win-win." My response back, "It is! I'll be bringing 20 years of expertise to your audience, and that will be your win." He ultimately agreed, and it was an incredibly successful event for both of us.

What is one bold action you can take today? This week? This month? This year?

What makes YOU stand out? The simple answer is reflected in the unique combination of what defines you, how others experience you, your strengths and your values. Incorporate this clarified Identity into your brand to more easily attract your ideal clients. When you are clear about who you are and what you can accomplish, your customers will reap the rewards, too.

Chapter Three
Key Two: Image

-3-

Key Two: Image

*"The beauty of a woman is not in a facial mode,
but the true beauty in a woman is in her soul."*

Audrey Hepburn

Education and experience are important, but a polished image also weighs very heavily in creating a favorable first impression. How you act, look and speak are often the most important in that one-tenth of a second it takes for someone to make a judgment about you. Key 2 to a profitable personal brand is your Image, your visual voice.

As a business owner, you are always "on". You never know who you'll run into that could end up being a new business relationship. For me, this point crystallized at my granddaughter's 5th birthday party. It was a Saturday, the weather was overcast, and I wasn't in the best of moods, but I anticipated that spending the afternoon with a room full of 5-year-olds and their parents might be a hoot. I fought the urge to give in to the weather, my mood and the informality of the occasion, and I prepared for the event with intention. I put on something colorful and polished. The day continued with children's party games, presents, and cake. I did my grandmotherly duties: socialized, helped where I could and cheered for my granddaughter on her special day. As fate would have it, one of the mothers in attendance was an executive from The Disney Company. Because I was prepared, I saw an opportunity to make a business connection that eventually resulted in a speaking engagement for me at Disney. Now had I let the weather, my mood, or the informality of the event sway me from showing my best self, that connection might not have ended so positively.

Planning Matters

Have you ever walked into a room and felt insecure about what you were wearing? Worried that your roots were showing? Wishing you had planned a little better so you would feel more confident? This is where good planning comes into play.

I had just begun my work with Helen, and I invited her to attend a conference with me. When she arrived, she confessed that she had been up late the night before, had way too much to drink, and then had been running late that morning. So she wore something comfortable—very loose and all black. As the conference began, she presented her business and made connections with other professionals. She soon became aware that she wasn't exuding confidence or feeling her power. Since Helen had allowed her current mood and unfortunate situation to determine her wardrobe choices, she hadn't dressed with intention for the statement she wanted to make at the conference. She hadn't planned her wardrobe in advance.

To avoid those last minute problems, once a week I take the time to plan my wardrobe for the upcoming week and make grooming appointments. Each Saturday once I've made my bed, turned on some jazz, made my coffee and pulled out my calendar, I plan for the upcoming week. I create my wardrobe ensembles (accessories and all) and hang them as outfits. When I'm in a relaxed state of mind, I'm more creative about my choices, and it's much more enjoyable. This crucial planning means no more pulling something together last minute only to realize that my jacket is missing a button, or the shirt needs ironing so that I have to go back to square one because I don't have time to take care of the problem. Planning gives you not only the opportunity to be sure your clothing is clean and pressed, but also time to make certain you have the proper undergarments for each look and that your shoes are polished to a shine.

When choosing your looks for the upcoming week, it's also important to think about how your clothing can transition with you as you move throughout your day -- from business meetings, to volunteer events, to a networking happy hour or a business dinner with your spouse. Based on your plans, you can dress a classic outfit up or down with the right add-on pieces or accessories. Knowing exactly what you'll be wearing is a confidence booster in and of itself.

Now, take a grooming inventory. What is the state of your hair, nails, skin and brows? Is it time to make some appointments in advance so you'll be looking your very best for that business conference or speaking engagement in three weeks?

Self-Care

Have you ever met someone who's well put together, but you can tell they're unhealthy, stressed, tired and unhappy? What they have is a misaligned image, one that's only skin deep. Successful personal image development requires a holistic approach. As women, we are taking care of everyone else and forgetting about ourselves. Then, when we do take "me" time, we feel guilty (or is it just me?). A routine of nutrition, exercise, sleep and quiet time is what helps us to be grounded, vibrant and successful women!

Self-care is the foundation of your image. My mother taught me to eat a healthy breakfast and yours may have, too. Of course, one of the reasons she did was because it was important to fuel my body with good food to begin my day. As it relates to your image, adapt the same philosophy. Just like eating a healthy breakfast to begin the day, what we do, see and say during the first part of our day is essential to our health, happiness and well-being.

Years ago, I would turn on the news first thing in the morning. That habit had me listening to news about killings, fires, traffic and other societal tragedies. Eventually, I realized I was filling my head with negative thoughts and emotions. I now listen to uplifting music and have a practice of prayer and meditation to begin my day balanced and centered. Then it's on to exercise and healthy nutrition. I've begun my day filling my mind, heart and body with positive thoughts and practices.

Now let's talk about how to close your day. Think of it as preparing for a positive sleep experience. Are you watching programs that may be sad or violent? Consider what that may be doing to your psyche while you sleep. My bedtime routine focuses on relaxing my mind and body. I stretch, take a warm scented bath (my favorite is lavender essential oils) and snuggle in my bed with an excellent book that will create a positive mindset before I drift off to sleep. Something like Chicken Soup for the Pet Lover's Soul by Jack Canfield, Mark Victor Hansen, and Carol Kline or The Happiness Advantage by Shawn Achor.

Your Wardrobe & Brand Alignment

The presenter, a well-known speaking coach, took the stage with his dress shirt tucked in on one side but not the other, and he was wearing a rumpled jacket. Then he actually drew attention to it, commenting on the fact that it was wrinkled because he had been traveling. As you might imagine, I was distracted by his haphazard appearance. The speaker went on to talk about first impressions as a speaker and how to gain instant credibility. On that day, what came out of his mouth was not in alignment with his appearance.

When the woman behind me whispered to her friend that she couldn't believe his shirt wasn't tucked in and wanted to fix it for him, I knew I wasn't the only one distracted. Because the audience was distracted, we were not able to absorb his message. You see, his wardrobe was not an accurate representation of his message, and that created a disconnect, an inconsistency.

When it comes to client attraction, looking your best is crucial and your wardrobe is a key element of that. Your potential client or boss is forming an opinion about you within a split second, and your visual voice (or image) speaks volumes. What is yours saying?

My client Linda (whom I previously mentioned) is also an example of how your wardrobe is connected to your brand identity. Remember, Linda is the whole earth nutritionist who promotes a vegan lifestyle for health reasons and because kind treatment of our earth and animals is a mission of hers. When building out her wardrobe, Linda made a point to stay away from leather shoes, handbags, etc. It was a great insight on her part. She represents her belief system throughout. What she wears aligns with her vegan lifestyle practices. This detail is significant in effectively aligning her self-packaging with her brand concepts.

Dress For the Client You Want to Attract

If you want to attract your ideal clientele, it's important that you dress as their peer. Mark Zuckerberg is a great example. A hoodie and jeans combo worked for him initially because he wanted to attract college students. It continues to work for him because he has an established personal brand. But when he began running in more influential crowds, he strategically began wearing suits when the occasion called for it--a smart move.

In my own experience, I've had numerous clients say that one of the reasons they were attracted to working with me is because I set the example of a powerful personal brand and dress the part. My look is classic with a kick. I wear neutral, classic clothing dressed up with bright funky accessories. It may seem obvious for me to look the part because it's my area of expertise. I am my own walking billboard, but so are you. Whether you are a CPA or social media expert, your visual representation is a valuable marketing asset. So when you show up polished and put together, you will attract the high-paying clients who will invest the big bucks your products and services are worth.

Wardrobe Essentials

Let's begin with the fundamental question of, "What are wardrobe essentials?" Your wardrobe essentials are the necessary foundations of building out a well-rounded trousseau: They are solid, neutral slacks, skirts, blazers, blouses, dresses, and coats. Wearing solid, neutrals keeps your look more classic, businesslike and gives you great versatility. Bear in mind that building a strong foundation is not about having lots of clothes but about having the right clothes.

If you're not the kind of person who is concerned with following seasonal trends and instead strives for some sort of continuity from year to year, you might gravitate toward a simple, classic wardrobe. Classics are timeless. The image portrayed with classic style is elegant, professional, no-nonsense and reflects leadership.

Color and Cut

Color is the most powerful element in your wardrobe and your personal brand. Wearing shades that flatter your coloring makes you look younger and healthier. Your eye color pops and your teeth look whiter. Knowing your palette also helps you build out a well-rounded wardrobe. Further, if you're an entrepreneur and building out a brand, you can create brand consistency by branding yourself in colors that flatter you and evoke emotion and action. While there are many philosophies in the psychology of color in marketing, remember that as an entrepreneur, people are buying because of you and what you reflect. Wouldn't it then make sense to put yourself in your best light?

If you're not sure what your best colors are, take a look at my mobile app *Color Rx* or my *Transformational Style Program* (http://www.TheTotalPackageBook.com/gifts). You will find that when you wear the colors that flatter you, you will garner more attention, be taken more seriously and perhaps best of all, you will feel more confident.

My client Susan loved to wear neutrals, but the wrong neutrals. The winter whites and browns she gravitated toward made her look sickly and her skin sallow. Together she and I worked on finding her best colors. Colors that made her look vibrant. She turned out to be a Winter—looking best in black and white accented with vibrant reds and turquoise. Once Susan was clear on her colors, she was able to build her wardrobe with intention, knowing that the neutrals she chose would not only look great on her but match with all of the pop colors in her palette, too.

It's also crucial to understand the cuts that will flatter your Body Silhouette because great fit is the sign of a well-dressed woman, and no matter how you're feeling about your body, you can feel beautiful in the right clothes! If you'd like to take a deep dive into the colors, cuts and styles that are right for you, take a look at my Transformational Style Program.

http://www.TheTotalPackageBook.com/gifts

Take Inventory

Once you've identified your best colors and cuts, begin by taking all of the blazers (then skirts, slacks, dresses, blouses, and coats) out of your closet and lay them on your bed. Ask yourself these 7 questions:

Is it a good color? If not, donate it.

Does it fit perfectly? If not, and you LOVE it, get it altered.

Is the style current? If it's looking dated or stuck in an era, donate it.

Is it clean and wrinkle-free? If not, wash, dry-clean and/or press.

Does it need mending? If so, time to pull out the sewing kit or drop it off at your tailor shop.

Is it in good condition (not tired and faded)? Remember, if you wear clothing that looks old and tired, that's exactly the way you'll feel... old and tired.

Does it match with at least three other things in your wardrobe? If not, you'll need to pick up a couple of items that compliment it which will create versatility.

Once you've completed this exercise, you should easily be able to create your shopping list. In my **Transformational Style Program**, I go into detail on what a complete wardrobe entails. Here is a quick list of the (minimum) basics as you begin to build a wardrobe: two coats, two sweaters, one pant or skirt suit, two blazers, two blouses, four tops, two skirts, three pants, one dress and four pair shoes.

Buy Quality

Your wardrobe essentials are investment pieces. They are timeless, and you want them to last. Don't be fooled though… just because something is pricey does not make it good quality. Look for fabrics that feel great and don't wrinkle. My favorite textiles are from England, Italy, and Spain.

My client Marian was focused on having as many clothes as possible but was discouraged that the items she was buying were not lasting. There was one skirt in particular that she wore once, cleaned per the instructions and it literally came apart at the seams. It turned out that she had a number of pieces that looked old and tired even though she had only worn them a few times. If she had invested in quality fabrics and craftsmanship, this wouldn't have happened.

How do you find quality?

First check the seams to be sure they lay flat and are finished on the inside of the garment. If you are looking at a print, be sure it matches at the seams. Are the buttons good quality or cheap plastic? Look at the fine details like the stitching around button holes. That alone will tell you a lot.

Then you can try my wrinkle test. Take a fistful of fabric and hold tightly for 15 seconds. When you let go, what does the fabric look like? If it quickly wrinkles and creases, you'll know that is exactly what it will look like once you've worn it a few minutes.

When building your collection of essentials, I suggest visiting stores that have complimentary personal shopping services so you will be guided to the designers that work for your Body Silhouette. Stores like Nordstrom, Bloomingdales, Macy's, Neiman Marcus and Saks.

Get the Matching Piece

Deborah had lots of quality clothing pieces but felt like she never had anything to wear. Once we had inventoried her clothing, it became very clear she had purchased lots of separates, but nothing really matched. Once she began to shop for her essentials with the intention of always having at least three pieces that matched, her problem was solved. Getting dressed became more streamlined, and packing for business trips became a snap.

If you are looking at suiting items, I strongly suggest you get the matching piece (even if you like to mix and match). That way you'll always have something that matches it. When you shop, take a look at how the item is displayed. Have they created your ensemble for you? If you love it, go for it- head to toe!

Identify Your Best Designers

One of the key questions I ask my clients is, "What designers work for you?" If you're not sure, visit your closet and look for the designers that repeat themselves. Those are your go-to brands so stick with them and then add a new one or two to expand. When I suggested this to my client Liza, she was thrilled to realize she didn't need to go back to square one each time she shopped. She knew she could rely on certain designers to work each time. By adding two new designers, we were able to broaden her selection while narrowing the shopping field. Also, because designers can come and go, Liza does not have all of her proverbial 'style' eggs in one basket.

Some of my favorite designers are: Lafayette 148, Classiques Entier by Nordstrom, Max Mara and Tahari. I prefer their clean, classic lines made in quality fabrics. Each of these designers has consistent craftsmanship and sizing. So rather than wandering through the women's clothing section, I head straight for these designers. If I need a dress, I can pull one out and know that the lines, fit and fabric will work for me. And best of all, the piece will last.

Now I'd love to be able to wear Banana Republic clothing, but their cuts don't work for my Body Silhouette. If you have a Round Body Silhouette, you might prefer Eileen Fisher and Chicos. So look for the designers whose clothing works best for your Body Silhouette and Style Essence (or personality).

Your Tailor is Your Friend

Tailored clothing will take your wardrobe a step further. Women in leadership like Sheryl Sandberg and Maria Shriver know that simple, classic lines reflect a level of professionalism and attention to detail. Having said that, it's important to remember that ready to wear clothing is cut for a specific Body Silhouette and may need some fine tuning. Alterations are your best friend in achieving a chic look that was made just for you.

Donna is one of my petite clients who was very resistant to investing in alterations. Once she became willing to having her pieces altered, she realized that her clothing choices expanded greatly, and she felt much more confident in her 'custom' clothes.

Keep it Classy (and not too sexy)

Have you ever encountered a professional woman whose cleavage was distracting? It's harder for women to know what to wear in the workplace because our culture has become so relaxed about workplace attire. The 20- and 30-somethings have been raised in the Casual Friday Era and can be confused about what is appropriate. However, showing too much in the workplace is always a big no! It's inappropriate for a business environment.

Without exception, every dress code I have read addresses the very sensitive topic of 'too sexy.' One male client specifically asked me to address it in my presentation to his employees. It's difficult, with the threat of sexual harassment, to speak to female employees about skirts that ride too high or outrageous platform heels meant for clubbing. Think of the time and resources businesses are wasting on this topic alone.

Studies show that a woman whose work attire is too provocative can be sabotaging her career. Further, women in high-level positions who dress in what is viewed as "sexy" outfits are considered less competent, regardless of their skill sets. Business etiquette experts say unflattering assumptions are made about women who wear provocative clothes, and those women are not taken seriously.

Last year I worked with Madeline, a stunning client who had a tendency to dress very sexy. When I met her, she was wearing a very low cut white blouse with a lacy black bra peeking through and a super short black pencil skirt over stiletto black patent leather pumps. Granted, she's a successful insurance agent, and she was looking to up-level her personal brand and increase business. She often works with couples and had indicated that women seem to be put off by her. I explained (right or wrong) that some women would be intimidated by her. Did her female clients feel uncomfortable discussing auto insurance while their husband's eyes strayed to Madeline's cleavage? I'd venture to say some couples stayed a mile away from Madeline because of it. Unfortunately, she was not willing to give up her low cut tops, too short skirts, and platform heels to up level her business. I wonder how much business she is still missing out on?

Some women are tempted to use their sexiness to advance their career. A woman should never resort to being sexy in order to get ahead in business. She should focus on the quality of her work and maintain a polished and professional personal style in a business setting. A woman's work wardrobe should complement who she is, not be distracting or send the wrong message that may hurt her career.

Now Accessorize

Now let's get creative with colors, textures and shapes, but be sure those adornments don't overpower your look. If you're artistic, you can easily pair a funky scarf with an otherwise simple look. If you're like me and love statement pieces, add a chunky necklace that steals the show. If you're the Grace Kelly type, pearls it is. The beauty of dressing classically is that you can express your individuality and style personality based on the accessories you choose.

Your accessories are more than necklaces, earrings and scarves. Keeping your brand colors and style in mind, a quality pen, watch, handbag, briefcase, notebook, or even phone cover can add power to your look. One of my dear friends and colleagues, Rona was always in black and white. I suggested she begin to add a pop of red to her look. Stepping out boldly, she bought herself a pair of red glasses, and now Rona's friends, clients and fans identify her with that pop of red. She's even had people stop her in airports to compliment her red glasses. Now whenever I see something with a splash of red, I think of my sweet friend Rona.

Recently I began working with a high-end bridal company that wanted to elevate its brand. The employees are known for wearing all black. At first I wasn't too thrilled with this concept, but then I heard their rationale. When helping a bride choose the perfect dress for her big day, their team doesn't want to clash or deter from the bride in any way. By dressing in all black, which is what most grooms will be wearing, their stylists, in essence, complement the bride during the selection process. A brilliant insight on their part! So when I went for our first training session, I too wore all black because I wanted to show up as one of their team members. I took it a step further and strategically added my signature style by wearing a chunky turquoise necklace. That pop of color and style wove my own brand identity into theirs. As I worked with the team, I encouraged each member to add their own subtle pop of color or stylish accessory to make a fashion forward statement while still maintaining the uniform.

What signature style will you choose so that people will begin to identify you with it?

Stay Current

Keeping your look current reflects that you stay current, period. An outdated wardrobe, hairstyle or makeup can prevent you from moving forward in your career. While it may seem subtle, looking current is a sign that you are current in your field of expertise. That doesn't mean to dive head first into the latest fads because frequently it's just a subtle change that is needed.

Alisha wanted to look more fashion forward but didn't wish to make any drastic changes. She had a great pixie haircut, so a simple change was in how she styled it. Instead of curling her hair under, she tried curling it up and brushing her bangs to the side. The small change made a huge difference. The same cut went from ho-hum to pow! Alisha looked chic and younger.

Is it time to update your hair and makeup? My personal clients know that an annual style, hair, and makeup audit is a must in keeping things current.

Personal Grooming

Dressing for success is more than just choosing the right outfit. To complete your professional look, you should also consider your personal grooming. Personal grooming is focused on subtleties that enhance and polish your appearance.

Rita was constantly battling gray roots because she only wanted to visit her hair stylist once every eight weeks. I explained that bumping her visits up to every four weeks and having fresh color was an investment in a reflection that she was 'on top' of things.

- Keep your hair cut, color and style fresh and current
- Keep your nails well-manicured, simple and business appropriate
- Keep your skin healthy and brows shaped
- Keep your makeup clean, simple and appropriate for daytime. Wearing too much is worse than none at all.
- Keep your scent VERY subtle, if at all. Avoid wearing perfume and heavily- scented products in business settings. One theory is that no one should be able to smell your scent unless they are 8" or closer to you.

Demonstrating that you care about your personal appearance communicates to your clients or audience that they are important to you, that you also will pay close attention to business details and the needs of your customers and clients.

Your Workspace

Your image is revealed through the state of your workspace and your car, too. Sound farfetched? Consider this. One of my colleagues is a job recruiter and routinely uses personal appearance to judge organizational skills. If she knows where her potential employee is parked, she sends someone to take a look at their car to see if it looks clean and orderly. Again, a reflection on how they will handle business. The old saying, "You can't judge a book by its cover" is true, and book jacket and product packaging experts have created an industry betting that people do judge and purchase products based on how they look.

If you work virtually and utilize live video chats, it's important that your workspace is branded, too. Consider what others will see when they see your workspace. For those of you who utilize your personal vehicle in your business, there's always a chance your clients will see it. So the state of your workspace or car needs to reflect the professionalism you want to deliver. Remember, the focus is on creating brand consistency and your workspace(s) ought to demonstrate the fine details of your business practice. Gain the non-verbal advantage by fully looking the part of success.

In the process of designing my new office, we have carefully planned a branding wall that will be the backdrop for my video chats, photographs, and video clips. This wall will be a light neutral color with a framed company logo in the center and a credenza topped with a few selected items that represent the tools of my trade, like my Transformational Style Guide, along with a fresh flower arrangement that compliments my branding colors. So why don't you take a step out in front of your workspace or car and examine them through the eyes of your clients. I'm sure it will be a revelation that will motivate some distinctive changes.

And More Planning

One of my big pet peeves is when I have an appointment with someone who consistently shows up late and complains about the horrible traffic (which I just drove through but arrived in a timely manner because I allowed plenty of lead time). Then s(he) sits down to start the meeting and asks, "Do you have a pen?" or announces, "I can't find my reading glasses." I do understand that things come up which prevent us from being prepared and on time, but that should not be a way of life or a consistent business pattern.

One of the things that my team member Jillian and I do at the beginning of each week is look at my calendar so that we can plan for my meetings. We pack a bag specifically for each meeting. We even upload the address into my navigation so that I'll know how much time I'll need to get to my appointment in a timely manner. My briefcase always has a pen, reading glasses, plenty of business cards and all the other accoutrements that I need to make a seamless presentation. This preparation lets my clients and business associates know that I honor and respect their time as well as my own.

Is your purse a disaster or your briefcase overflowing with unorganized papers? As a successful professional, paying attention to the details is not optional; it speaks volumes about how you will care for your clients. Not only are these preparations good for business, but they are also essential for your own sense of self. There is nothing more frustrating than looking in my purse and not finding what I need, so that's why cleaning out my purse and briefcase is another task accomplished weekly at this prep time. Think of how nice it would be to know that when you arrive at a meeting, you are so confident and prepared, you can fully focus on the important business at hand.

Your polished Image is crucial to your business success. It is reflected in your wardrobe as well as your workspaces and your attention to organization details. All of these present The Total Package. Each is a piece of the puzzle that will seem unfinished if missing. Beyond that, you are caring for yourself, and you will benefit from more confidence and higher self-esteem. What better way to shine than from a glow that radiates from within?

Chapter Four
Key Three: Language

-4-
Key Three: Language

*"Without language, one cannot talk
to people and understand them;
one cannot share their hopes and
aspirations, grasp their history,
appreciate their poetry, or savor
their songs."*

Nelson Mandela

None of us will know when the first story was told. It could have been in a dark cave or possibly sitting on a rock by a rushing river. While we may never know, it's important to remember that it was spoken and subsequently written language that allowed lessons, fables, and history to be communicated.

Language is one of the things that sets us apart as beings, one of the things that essentially defines us as humans. Language, when used well, can bring about very deep feelings. It can inspire us to take bold actions and it can set the tone for our relationships.

Identity Language

In the first section of this book I focused on developing your brand persona—your identity, which helped you gain clarity about how to communicate from your strengths and uniqueness. Language is a fantastic way to weave who you are, what you stand for and what you value into your marketing, branding, communications and social media presence.

Once I had established my own personal brand identity through the exercises and assessments I highlighted in Key One: Identity, I began to weave my brand persona language throughout my brand in order to create a cohesive and consistent experience. I started use terms like elite, strategic, connected, exemplary, care, invested, activate, relate, passionate, proven and dynamic- to name a few.

Without a doubt, when I became clear about staying on target with my own brand identity language, I began attracting the attention of the clients I envisioned working with.

Wrong Language

Ten of us were standing in a cluster at a networking conference, and it was time to do the structured interactive exercise. Each of us had 5 minutes to describe our business, target market and ask for something specific from the group. The fourth to go was Bob, well dressed with an air of confidence and a big smile. As he began to speak there was a drastic shift in the energy of the group because within his first few sentences he used profanity 3 times and his grammar was atrocious. His appearance was just right but then he opened his mouth, and it was clear from the comments of others (after the fact) that his language had hurt his personal brand and reputation.

Language is a very powerful tool. How we use language shapes our world both internally and externally. How you deliver communication shapes the way the world sees you. How you express yourself with your spoken or written word has the power to instantly connect you to others or turn them off as Bob had. If you think that cursing in a professional setting is harmless, think again: using foul language in business may also be harming your career.

My extensive research into studies on this topic revealed that a majority of employers said they'd be less likely to promote someone who curses on the job. Further, a vast majority believe that when employees swear at work, it makes them appear less professional, and shows lack of control and maturity. It even makes them seem less intelligent.

The good news is, speaking in a calm, concise and professional manner, without any of the @#!%, leaves a positive impression on colleagues and clients.

Weak Language

Have you ever met someone who is so polite you wonder what the catch is? Possibly someone who always apologizes for no apparent reason other than they want to be liked? Or is it subtle language that keeps expressing, "My opinion isn't important"? Do you know someone like that? Is that someone you?

The ability to communicate effectively and confidently has a dramatic effect on the capacity to advance your career. You may fall into the trap of using weak language that sabotages your efforts to present yourself with authority and confidence.

In the past few years, women have been called out on an issue that is a subtle, yet not so subtle one. It began with a provocative Pantene Ad campaign showing women in a constant state of apology. A woman seated in a business meeting, "Sorry, may I ask a question?" A woman poking her head in an office, "Sorry, do you have a moment to talk?" A woman sitting in a waiting room and when another sits next to her and bumps her arm, the seated woman apologizes. Universally, women who viewed the video were struck with, "I do this all the time", but most were not even aware of it. Whether we are asking a question or walking down a crowded sidewalk, we seem to feel the need to apologize well... just for existing.

The ad suddenly shifts gears and shows women who are strong, taking control and still doing so in a polite manner. "Sorry, may I ask a question?" shifts to "My question is..." The ad's empowering message is Don't Be Sorry, Be Strong and Shine. Generally, women tend to have more of a right brain, left brain connection and because of that, we tend to be sensitive and apologize often.

Research shows that women consistently apologize more than men, and that makes us appear weak and that the simple five letter word S-O-R-R-Y has a significant impact on how we are perceived. Moving forward, if we can delete the apology and move forward with our statement or question, we will be seen as more powerful, confident and accomplished.

Another poignant example of weak language has been highlighted in a number of recent articles. The word 'just' is weakening the position of women in the workplace.

This topic first came to light because of Google and Apple alum Ellen Petry Leanse. She noticed that women were using the word 'just' much more than men. Petry Leanse stated, "'Just' wasn't about being polite, it was a subtle message of subordination and deference..., striking it from a phrase clarified the request and made it more powerful."

I must admit, it has been an ongoing challenge (but a fun one) for me to become more aware of the language I use that weakens my communications. Take the challenge yourself; become mindful of the language you are using. Remove the verbiage that is weakening your position and you'll be amazed at the results.

Powerful Language

Finally, let's address the importance of powerful language. Use of language that is clear, concise and strong will bolster the opinion others have of you.

One of my favorite television shows is about a woman, new to politics. In one episode, her campaign manager was coaching her on how to ask for the financial support and endorsement of a highly influential voter. The candidate first tried, "Mr. Smith, I hope you will support my campaign." Her handler went on to explain that the word 'hope' was weakening her request. He went on to advise her to make, what ended up being, her ultimate request, "Mr. Smith, I want your endorsement and financial support." Keeping her request succinct and direct was much more powerful and ultimately ended up winning the voter's support. Granted, this is a television show, but the point is well taken.

While it may seem subtle, the words "I think", "I feel", and "I hope" can introduce doubt to your audience. The stronger options like, "I'm convinced" or "I'm confident" will bolster your request. Removing the words altogether can emphasize that strength even more.

Take a look at these examples:

Weak: "I think it would be a good idea."
Strong: "I'm convinced it's a good idea."
Strongest: "It is a good idea."

Weak: "I feel this is the right networking organization for you."

Strong: "I'm confident this is the right networking organization for you."

Strongest: "This is the right networking organization."

Have you ever wanted someone to get to the point or were lost about the context of what they were trying to communicate? Being on point and creating context is powerful language. I was speaking with Karen at a business conference, and it was clear she had a specific request, but I wasn't able to pin it down. She was talking in circles, explaining herself, using apologetic language and finally I had to ask her, "What is your specific request, Karen?" If she had made her desire known and set the context in the beginning, I would've been able to consider more seriously her request.

Further, brevity matters and keeping your business conversations succinct and clear will make you stand out as a leader. Muddling your points with too much information can confuse the audience and cause them to lose interest. Also, too much of an explanation or taking too long getting to the point dilutes the very point you're trying to make. Be direct and upfront when communicating, even if you're having a difficult conversation or offering constructive feedback.

Your Elevator Pitch (The Flirt Factor)

No, not the kind you're thinking of! Bear with me here. I approached Deena at a networking event, introduced myself and asked her name and about her career. She paused, looked up at the ceiling and responded, "I bring a complete sense of calmness to the life of busy professionals." Hmmmm? Was she a massage therapist, a psychologist, an esthetician? It turned out she was a professional organizer. How would I have known?

I do realize that the pressure to deliver in such a short period of time can be daunting. As a professional speaker, I'd much rather have 90 minutes to present than the time crunch of making the right first impression with a short description of who I am and what I offer. Just thinking about it makes my heart pound!

Your elevator pitch is a brief interaction and time to say just enough or 'flirt' so that it will compel others to know more about you. It's not the time to thoroughly educate others or describe your business philosophy. It is not an opportunity to go into detail about all of your products and services. It is a time to express who you are, the problem you solve, who your target market is, and what you offer.

Deena would have been more effective had she elaborated a little more… "I bring calmness to the life of busy professionals through streamlining and organizing offices and routines."

Business professionals have been taught they need to have an elevator pitch, but many haven't crafted one in a way that sounds natural and non-rehearsed. It's important to be sure yours does not sound synthetic and filled with your industry's jargon. When I hear one like that, in my mind I'm hearing, blah, blah, blah.

Also, be aware of your audience. If you're at a networking event for corporate professionals, and you initially developed your pitch for entrepreneurs, you'll want to modify it to say business professionals, not entrepreneurs.

Once you land on your ideal pitch, don't get too stuck on it. As you evolve, your pitch should evolve, too. Keeping it fresh creates engagement and can attract someone you've known for years, but had not yet communicated to them with your evolved language.

Your pitch can be a question. A clothing stylist might say, "Do you open the doors to a closet full of clothes and still feel like there's nothing to wear? My services take you from Ugh, what am I going to wear to what do I get to wear?"

Practice your pitch and get feedback from trusted professionals. It may sound good to you but may come across as too polished or not conversational. Remember, people work with you because they connect with you, not because you made a point to sell all of your benefits.

Non-Verbal Language

Posture

Sara's parents had splurged on the perfect wedding. She had spent months searching for a silk wedding gown in winter white. In the weeks leading up to the big day, she had done a trial run with her hair and makeup. Her fingernails and toenails were polished with a color aptly named Wedding Day.

The air was crisp, the sun shining and the breeze just right for this early fall outdoor wedding. The wedding march began, and we stood with anticipation as the blushing bride began walking down the aisle with her father firmly by her side. All of the pieces were in place, but when Sara began to move towards the front of the room, there was a complete disconnect between the celebration of the day and her closed up posture. Yes, she had a smile on her face, but her shoulders were hunched and her head down. I wanted to rush to her side and whisper in her ear that this was HER day and she should stand tall and claim it with every fiber of her being.

Body language is nonverbal, but it communicates volumes about you nonetheless. Professor Emeritus of Psychology at UCLA, Dr. Albert Mehrabian teaches that, "Communication is 55% body language, 38% tone of voice and 7% words." So how you carry yourself when engaged in conversation, enter a room or step onto a stage is often as important, if not more important than what you say.

Mastering your non-verbal communication can increase your income and ultimately attract your ideal clientele. Much of our body language is instinctive, changes how others see us and also how we see ourselves. Confident and powerful body language will make you more effective at networking, increase sales effectiveness, elevate your influence and give your business the non-verbal edge.

This is also evident in the research and teaching of Harvard Social Psychologist and TED Talk phenomenon Amy Cuddy, author of Presence: Bringing Your Boldest Self to Your Biggest Challenges. Cuddy shows how "power posing" — standing with confident and open posture (even when we're not feeling very confident) can affect the testosterone and cortisol levels in our brain. The powerful position can increase testosterone levels that result in a sharp, clear mind and may also decrease cortisol levels that can reduce stress and nervousness. No doubt these physiological benefits will affect your success.

Body orientation is also important. This is the degree to which one's shoulders, legs and feet are turned toward, rather than away from the other. Being that I am a body language nerd (I really do love observing people) I became aware of the fact that people tended to engage more with those who were facing them directly than they did with those whose body language was pointing even slightly away. I even did my own mini research. While speaking with another business owner, I noticed that although I was facing her straight on, she began ever so slowly to shift to the side. When I subtly adjusted my stance to face her, she shifted again. It made her appear uncomfortable and insecure.

Also, open body positions are perceived more positively than closed body positions. Open positions can be knees slightly apart, legs stretched out, elbow away from the body, hands not touching, legs uncrossed. People with open body positions are more persuasive than those with closed body positions.

When I was coaching my client Dee on her non-verbal language, I observed that her position was open, but her upper torso was leaning slightly back, or away from the individual she was interacting with. I explained that it was reflecting an insecure, defensive or even a standoffish energy. When she began to lean in slightly, she reported that people seemed to be more relaxed and talkative with her.

As an adolescent, my mother reminded me to stand up straight, and of course, I rolled my eyes as most teens would. One day we were sifting through some pictures we took on our recent vacation to Arizona and there I was, slouching terribly. It was then that I took heed of her advice and began to be aware of my posture.

Great posture takes commitment. My regular practice of Pilates is a big part of that commitment. I have also made a point to sit at my desk in a healthy posture (BTW I just adjusted it as I sit here writing :)). The driver's seat of my car is set in a way that promotes good posture as well. I've even chosen someone to visualize as my reminder. Robin Wright's character Claire Underwood in House of Cards carries herself regally, with confidence and grace. Each time my posture needs adjustment, I think of her.

If you're speaking, making a pitch, interviewing for a job or attending a business event, I suggest power-posing for a couple of minutes before you enter. Think Wonder Woman's pose-feet firmly planted hip-width apart, shoulders back, head held high and hands on your hips. If you feel silly in this pose, just make a point to stand with very open body language, that of a winner. I'm not suggesting you carry one of those poses into your setting. Consider it your warm-up for success! I consistently power-pose before a presentation and take that a step further by doing a few jumping jacks (not too many or I'll run out of breath). It gets my blood going and my energy level up.

Pat McClenahan, President and CEO of the 2015 Los Angeles Special Olympics, described an amazing example of power posing and why it became the iconic logo that represented winners. "The mark that we ended up with is the celebratory figure of an athlete representing courage, determination, and joy." He went on to point out, "throughout history, in any culture when someone wins or celebrates, they raise their arms in the air and open their body language to that of a winner."

Eye Contact

Making direct eye contact with someone does most of the work in creating attraction and dramatically enhances other behaviors like smiling and listening.

Eye contact is the most immediate and noticeable nonverbal message. Not enough and you can seem untrustworthy and uninterested. Too much may seem inappropriate for most professional settings. In a business setting, long glances rather than intense stares are the most effective.

Eye contact is one of the easiest and most powerful ways to make a person feel important, valued and validated. Simply holding someone's gaze — whether it's a prospective client or a dear friend — has the power to create connectivity or deepen a relationship. It creates and increases attraction and according to research, holding someone's gaze has been proven to spark an unforgettable attraction. This is true in a business setting as well as romantic relationships.

To truly understand why eye contact is so important, we need to gain clarity in how central it is to the human experience. The results of a 2002 study revealed that an infant was much more likely to follow its parents' eyes than it was the movement of their head. A more primal example of how deeply rooted eye contact is in our DNA is to point out that in our cavemen ancestors, eye contact could mean the difference between life and death.

Making solid eye contact can make you more memorable because it can evoke a feeling. As Maya Angelou said, "I've learned that people will forget what you said, people will forget what you did, but people will never forget how you made them feel."

Keep in mind that cultures can vary drastically as it relates to non-verbal communication so carefully study the different customs of those with whom you conduct business.

Smile

Women, even more so than men, give greater weight to facial expressions and body language than we do to words. It's crucial to become self-aware not only of posture and eye contact but also of facial expressions. Your facial expressions even affect your tone of voice, yet another significant factor in your communication.

Decades of research prove that your mood is elevated and your stress is reduced if you smile, even for a short period of time. A full, true smile involves your eyes as well as your mouth. Smile even when you don't feel like it. It will improve the way others interact with you and pretty soon your smile will align with how you're feeling!

In business settings, your smile is an asset--a strong statement of confidence and approachability. Smiles have an enormous effect on the recipient. The presence of a smile (or not) provides a non-verbal signal that can be very telling in successful negotiations. Flashing your pearly whites can literally make other people feel like they are winning. Smiles are contagious and are often paid forward. When you smile at someone, they instinctively return that smile which makes both of you feel good.

Much of this is brain chemistry, but if you think about it... when you make others feel good, they want to be around you, and when they wish to be around you, they hire you!

In addition to being a naturally happy and optimistic person, I'm also very task oriented. When I'm in my 'task mode' I tend to focus in a way that makes me look serious. Others may perceive that I'm frowning, so I have become very self-aware of my facial expressions or smiles. Just as I do Pilates to strengthen my posture, I begin my day smiling at myself in the mirror to activate my own smile muscles. I also remind myself each morning that I will smile. I surround myself with happy people and visual reminders like quotes and pictures to bolster that reminder, too.

It all begins with a smile. My son is a voiceover actor and has taught me that speaking with a smile fully reflects the emotion of friendliness. Record your outgoing voicemail message while smiling. You'll be amazed at the difference in tone.

Handshake

A number of years ago I was equally considering two business coaches. They had similar areas of expertise, were well established and highly experienced. I was having a difficult time making the final choice and asked for one last face-to-face meeting with each one. Their handshakes were what broke the tie. The woman with the warm shake who looked me directly in the eye was hired. The other had a weak grip. I was looking for someone with confidence and the expert I ultimately chose communicated those qualities in the seconds it took to shake hands!

What is your handshake like? Is it weak, like steel or just the right amount of pressure? A solid, firm grip is ideal. If you're not sure what yours is like, I suggest practicing with a friend or family member. Keep yours brief (but not too brief) and straight up and down. If you struggle with sweaty palms, there are a number of medical remedies or you can subtly wipe your hand off on your pant leg (or skirt) right before you shake. Take your handshake to the next level and be sure to look the other person directly in the eye and smile. The connection will be a genuine and lasting one.

How important is a good handshake? Studies show that the amount of connection you get from a handshake can be equal to three hours of face time. For women, it is especially important to offer your hand when you first meet someone. While the male/female business relationship has highly evolved, men can still feel unsure if they should instigate the handshake or wait for the woman to do so.

How you communicate with others can be the difference between a successful connection and the loss of a customer. How you speak, write, carry and express yourself will be incredibly powerful elements in reflecting a profitable personal brand.

Chapter Five
Key Four: Online Presence

-5-

Key Four: Online Presence

"Make it simple. Make it memorable.
Make it inviting to look at."

Leo Burnett

Social Media Engagement

Your online engagement and posts are an opportunity to reflect YOU at YOUR best. Don't miss an ideal opportunity to lift and inspire others with content that does the same for you. This is the place to share all of the values you identified in the Key One: Identity. If your family is the center of your life, share your special occasions so your audience can cheer along with you. For me, the Salvation Army is dear, so I jump at every chance I get to promote their inspiring stories of generosity, love and hope.

By contrast, one of the biggest turnoffs in social media engagement is "the rant" or negative posts complaining about someone or something. Let me say this in the nicest way possible... NO ONE CARES and it turns your audience off. Negativity does just two things--it attracts others who are negative and repels the positive and uplifting ones.

Your social media engagement is also an effective way to align yourself with brands you love and attract their attention, too. Nordstrom (one of my happiest places on earth) is one of my previous employers and my go-to place to shop for myself, my family, and my clients. Whenever I get the chance to give Nordstrom a shout out I do. Aligning my business with a strong and consistent brand like Nordstrom is a subtle reflection that my brand is strong and consistent as well.

Education Based Marketing

Freely sharing your knowledge is also a great way to establish yourself as a leader in your industry by showcasing your expertise and your generosity with it. Education-based marketing (EBM) is a prime opportunity to deliver quality education and teach someone something that solves a real world problem–a problem currently keeping them up at night. What better way to establish yourself as a leader than to freely share your area of expertise? When you provide your potential clients with great information, you are establishing yourself as an experienced, smart, and resourceful person—and an authority in your field.

Another benefit of EBM is that it creates more informed customers who make more informed decisions. It's a time saver, too. If you've wasted far too many hours answering basic questions over and over again, create a website that develops more informed customers who already know the answers to frequently asked questions.

EMB is also a wonderful opportunity to represent your 'client-focused' approach. Instead of trying to get your audience to buy something, first understand that they have needs. Their first need when faced with a business challenge is accurate, precise information. Fill that need and they will likely trust you to help them further.

EMB is also search engine friendly. When people search for experts, they type in questions. They are looking for answers before they even become aware they need to hire you. Filling your site with information organically attracts search engine users and ultimately new clientele.

Your Photographs & Videos

Have you ever met someone who looked nothing like the picture on her website or marketing materials? Was her picture too posed? Was it outdated? Did it really reflect the truth of how she shows up in person? This is a personal brand snafu, to be sure. I know you've experienced it, too.

One of the benefits of an aligned, authentic and current digital representation is when people meet you in person, they will feel like they already know you. I was attending the eWomenNetwork annual conference last summer and during one session, a woman (I didn't know yet) sent me a Facebook message asking to meet for coffee during the break. She had heard about me from a mutual friend and had been observing me online to see if I might be a fit to speak for two conferences the following year. I spent a few minutes perusing her online presence before our live meeting and was able to quickly ascertain she was someone I should get to know. We instantly recognized each other because our profile pictures were current. Also, each of us had a true prior impression of what the other person was like and we were able to connect quickly face to face. I inked the speaking gigs within 15 minutes over coffee--definitely a record! Had our pictures been outdated or digitally enhanced to the extreme, our connection would not have been as powerful.

Just like a real-world first impression, the images/videos you use for your digital presence have the power to create an instant connection or turn your customers off. Professional images are not snapshots taken at a BBQ last weekend. Your professional images should be current, high quality and reflect the individuality of you. In a competitive market, any edge over your competition is worth activating. Whether you're an experienced corporate executive or a successful entrepreneur, a congruous online impression is a must. That presence plays a crucial role, and your photographs should reflect that you are an authority in your field and trusted professional.

My client Liz called one day to ask me if I knew anything about a man she was considering hiring to become her social media coach. I was not familiar with him and went to the first place I observe a professional, his Facebook page. When I clicked on his profile, the first thing that struck me was that his profile picture (on his business page) was one of him with his arm around his buddies--each of them sporting a cold beer. Although he may have been a spectacular social media coach, I couldn't get past his unprofessional image.

Your profile picture should be a high quality professional close-up headshot so your audience can look you in the eye. It's a first impression opportunity to represent the very best of you and your expertise in a visual element. I also suggest you use the same profile picture for all of your social media outlets, yet another opportunity to create personal brand consistency.

When it comes to your video presence, it's essential to keep your content current. Time after time I visit the sites of well-established professionals only to find that their photographs and videos are outdated--often by up to a decade! One such example was homepage video footage from the late 80's. The business coach that was the subject of the video had a dated hairstyle that required copious amounts of product (hello Aqua Net) and highly-teased bangs. She was sporting big shoulder pads and a neon orange blouse. Her frizzy hair and 80's fashion forward style were a good thing at the time, but the image it now reflected was actually working against her. Had nothing changed? Was her message even relevant?

In order to keep your personal brand fresh and contemporary, your images and videos should change ideally once a year or once every couple of years at the most. When your digital presence is outdated and tired, it's a reflection that you haven't kept up with the times or, to take that a step further, your offerings may not be relevant any longer.

Schedule an annual photo shoot for your web presence. These fresh images represent a constant evolution and the growth and success of your business. They create a curiosity, and your online audience will want to know what's new and exciting!

If it's been a while since you last looked at your own digital presence, take the time now to inventory it and mentally apply what you've learned. Elevating your digital impression could require a complete overhaul or it may mean just a few minor tweaks. Are there changes that need to be made? Possibly it's time to reach out to your marketing team, a terrific photographer- maybe even a personal branding expert! Hire a team who knows their stuff. Remember, this is a business investment and your chance to make a lasting first impression even before you meet your client. Yes, you do need a professional to do your styling, hair, and makeup. Someone who's highly experienced in her/his field. Over the top? I think not.

Photo/Video Shoot Checklist

Don't miss out on your chance to capture curiosity with your photos and videos. Developing a strong personal brand and visual voice that is well represented digitally creates that instant connection and compels prospective clients to click forward to learn more about you.

Any edge over your competition is worth activating. Whether you're an experienced corporate executive or a successful entrepreneur, a powerful and congruous online impression is a must. That presence plays a crucial role, and your photos/videos should reflect that you are a leader, the authority in your field and a trusted professional.

My experience shows that careful preparation for your shoot will have you showing up as you, at your very best, with the ability to be confident about why your people should choose to hire you over your competition. As you read on, keep in mind that while this checklist is specific to your video or photo shoot, it can be used for any special occasion, even if that particular occasion is your day to day life.

May I get on my beautifully branded soapbox for just a moment? Not all professionals are created equal. Hiring the best will clearly reflect in your personal brand and ultimately your overall brand presence. High-level videographers, photographers, makeup artists, hairstylists, personal brand and image experts (wink, wink), marketing experts and graphic artists are worth the investment in yourself and your success. Fully trust their process. It's one thing to make the $$ investment, but another altogether to TRUST that these professionals are truly able to see the full potential of you. Don't get in your own way. If you cut corners when you hire, it will show! I will step down from my soapbox now.

Let's begin! Before you tackle your checklist, take a look at the following countdown to get an idea of the sequencing, planning and prep work to be done. Remember...each and every checklist item is there for a reason. Although hair, makeup, and massage may seem like fluff, they are not. They are a comprehensive and strategic approach to building a success-ful brand and business.

Grooming

There is no detail too small when it comes to grooming. Everything counts! When you pay attention to the fine details of your image, it is a reflection that you are detail-oriented when it comes to your business too.

✔Calendar your appointments: Once you book your photo/video shoot, schedule your hair, nail, skin, and test-makeup appointments well in advance.

✔Hair: The ideal time to schedule your hair color and cut is two weeks to ten days prior to your shoot. Then your style will be fresh but still have the time to grow out just a tad, so it's looking and feeling very natural. Now is NOT the time to try a drastic change in cut or color. You may live to regret it.

✔Makeup: You may be great at doing your own makeup, but there is an art to makeup application for photo and video. Don't rely on yourself, your girlfriend or the random artist at the cosmetic counter. Hire an expert with substantial experience in video/photography makeup application. You'll be happy you did!!

✔Brows: Your eyebrows are the frame of your face and often neglected. The proper shape and color make your eye color POP! Ask your hair stylist for a reference to someone who is experienced at waxing and knows brows.

✔For the guys: Be sure your nose and ear hairs are trimmed (yes, I said that :). If you sport facial hair keep it neatly trimmed and shaped unless your brand speaks otherwise!

✔Nails: A mani-pedi is an excellent way to spend some downtime 2-3 days before your shoot. You can relax, and you'll be assured your nails will look great. Opt for a very neutral color because you want the focus to be on your beautiful face, not your grape purple nails.

✔Whiten Your Teeth: A white smile makes you look younger and more successful. If you are a regular whitener, do a re-fresh 1-2 days before your shoot. If you're a first-timer, begin your treatments at least a month prior. Talk to your dentist about the best teeth whitening solution for you.

✔Moisturizing: Dry skin can detract from looking your very best. 5-7 days before your shoot, be diligent in moisturizing your whole body. Add a good exfoliation every couple of days and your skin will glow!

✔Red Eyes: Put your eye drops in the refrigerator for a nice cool treatment first thing in the morning and right before you get your makeup done. Set your alarm for 20 minutes earlier and spend those first 20 with a bag of frozen peas (wrapped in a paper towel) on your eyes to take down any puffiness.

Self Care

While it would be ideal that your self-care routine be in place on a regular basis, I'm well aware that life can get in the way. Immediately begin to focus on your nutrition, water intake, exercise, sleep and quiet time. The good news is that you'll be creating a habit you can carry forward!

I am a firm believer in walking my talk, and at times, I really struggle remembering to put ME on my to-do list. If you are like me, you may want to reach out to an expert to support you in optimizing your health, so I ask for the support of a health coach, Pilates instructor, nutritionist, etc. A healthy individual is attractive and compelling and that, in and of itself, will mag-netize the business relationships and clients you want.

✔Nutrition: Avoid eating salty foods or anything that makes you bloat or causes gas.

✔Water: Substantially increase your water intake so you'll be well hydrated. Your skin will be supple, hair shiny, eyes glowing and your mind will be clear.

✔Avoid Alcohol: Limit your alcohol intake to little or no alcohol for 3-4 days leading up to your shoot. Although there are health benefits to your red wine, it can cause you to be puffy and look tired.

✔Exercise: Increasing your exercise will make you stronger, more confident, relaxed and will reflect vigor and vitality.

✔Sleep: Medical professionals will agree that getting plenty of sleep is anti-aging. In addition to all of the health benefits, solid sleep leading up to your shoot date (well, anytime) will clear your head, and your eyes will look less tired.

✔Quiet time: Take the time each day to reflect on the WHY of your business. Focusing on what motivates you will get you centered and be evident in your photos and videos.

Wardrobe

When you walk into a room, appear on a video, or step onto a stage, your visual presentation speaks volumes. Your audience forms an impression of you in the blink of an eye and a polished wardrobe is an essential element not to be ignored. Planning is crucial to reflecting a professional and successful image and in developing video and photos for your digital presence. The following checklist will help you plan for the ideal look(s) you want to achieve so that you'll feel fantastic!

✔Number of outfits: Begin by determining the number of outfits you'll need for your shoot date. Keep in mind that you can achieve an entirely different look by changing up just your top and accessories.

✔Solids: I strongly suggest you stick to solids. Prints and stripes can be tricky and often don't visually translate well on video or photos.

✔Color charisma: It is important to know your best colors and choose from the rich tones that work best for your natural coloring. If you're developing your brand, choose colors that look great on you and also communicate the message you want your brand to communicate. For instance, I use blue. Blue creates trust AND it's one of my best colors. Once you've determined your best colors on my Color Rx app, opt for rich tones in alignment with your brand, so the look is consistent, which creates credibility.

✔Fit: No matter how you're feeling about your body, you can look beautiful in clothes. Opting for cuts that flatter your body and fit you properly reflect an attention to detail and can make you look up to 15 pounds thinner. Be sure your clothes are the proper size for the body you have now. No one but you can see the size on your tag. If you're not sure what works for you, my Transformational Style Program will teach you the best cuts and necklines for your unique body silhouette.

✔Unmentionables: Be mindful of the undergarments you wear for your shoot. Be sure you have the right bra and foundation for each and every outfit. Worrying about constantly adjusting your bra straps, the color of your bra showing through your top or a little bulge interfering with a smooth fit distracts you from being the most confident version of you.

✔Jewelry: Choose jewelry that compliments your look but doesn't overpower it. If you'll be doing close-up work, I suggest shorter necklaces that flatter your neckline. Think V-neck, v-necklace. Round neck, round necklace. Get it?

✔Shoes: Shoes are a detail often forgotten. Be sure yours are polished, clean and look new. Maybe it's time to visit your local shoe-shine.

Once you've created your ensembles take extra care in pressing or steaming them and hang them as complete outfits, accessories and all. If you have some small drawstring bags, you can sort your accessories by outfit and hang them on the corresponding hanger. On the morning of your shoot, protect your outfits in zippered garment bags to keep them clean during transport.

Props

Your personal brand, marketing expert, videographer, and photographer are a great resource to brainstorm the best props to include in your shoot, but here is a suggestion: your book. If you have published a book or have a product for sale, be sure to bring it. It's important YOU be seen with it; then others will want it too.

Note: If you haven't published your book yet, but the cover design is complete, make a mock book cover and attach it to a hardback book. No one will know you're actually holding To Kill a Mockingbird. If the cover has not been designed, bring a book that is the same size as yours will be. Your graphic designer or photographer can always superimpose your cover once you have it.

✔Tools of the trade: Think about what you actually use in your area of expertise. A nutritionist might bring healthy food. A fitness coach could bring weights or exercise bands. A realtor could hold her iPad or a beautiful keychain with keys to just the right house.

Ok, now you're ready for your shoot!

There is only one unique and beautiful you. You were put on this earth with a powerful purpose and people need you, your services and products. Showing up with that belief, well prepared because of the above checklists, you'll be sure to shine your light!

Download your Photo/Video Shoot Checklist here:
www.TheTotalPackageBook.com/gifts

Chapter Six
Key Five: Customer Experience

-6-
Key Five: Customer Experience

*"One customer well taken care of could be
more valuable than $10,000 worth of advertising."*

Jim Rohn

The Antiguan sky was a vivid blue, accessorized with just a few billowing clouds. The azure sea filled the warm breeze with a tinge of salt as my husband Joe, and I headed to the hotel's quiet adults-only pool with the cascading waterfall. I walked up to the bar area to pick up towels for our lounge chairs only to find there were none left. When I asked the hotel attendant about it, her curt response was, "You'll need to get your towels at the main pool today. We don't have any here." If you're anything like me, the hair on the back of your neck just stood up.

Whether you know it or not, you are an expert on customer service. At one point or another during your day, you are a customer. You know good service when you see it, and you know bad service when you experience it like I did in Antigua. You don't need to read a book to have that explained to you. On one side of the business equation is you and the other side is your customer. You provide good products and services for a price. If there's a problem, you want to take care of it as quickly and seamlessly as possible. You want your customer happy. You already know this; so why is a great customer experience so elusive?

Your personal brand is your customer's overall experience of you. From their first impression to the follow-up and beyond can mean the difference between just satisfied clients and loyal customers who can't wait to rave about you--the difference between ordinary and extraordinary. Let's consider some top names in customer experience like Apple, Nordstrom, Disney, Starbucks and Zappos. My research found that these companies collaboratively learn from each other. Recently one of my clients, a renowned real estate developer in Los Angeles, was awarded Best Concierge Services in The Wall Street Journal. As I toured his properties, the director shared that they had learned elements of their valuable culture from Disney, and that ultimately, Disney executives had asked to visit their properties to gain access to their customer experience expertise. Each and every detail of the grounds was meticulously maintained--even the brass topped trash cans were polished to a shine. Clearly, they know manicured surroundings create an upscale and enjoyable experience for their customers.

You may be asking, what does this have to do with your personal brand? Sadly, there are many experts/businesses whose services and products are high quality, but they're missing the mark when it comes to the customer's experience. What might they be missing? It comes down to company culture and systemized implementation. Think of creating a serve-first, brand-aligned culture within your business, whether you're a solopreneur or have a team of 1,250. With every fine detail, ask yourself: Will this touch point serve and enhance my customer's experience? Will it make them feel valued? Is it brand aligned?

I am a fifth generation entrepreneur. I was taught the importance of the customer's experience from my father and mother. No doubt it had been passed down to them from both sets of grandparents, who also owned businesses. My parents owned a wheel alignment and brakes auto shop that was known for meticulous care, and its unofficial moniker was the cleanest shop in town. When you think of an auto repair business, what comes to mind? All mechanics are crooks? A dirty, greasy, smelly environment? Well, my parents knew they needed to deliver quality service, a relationship of trust, and a spotless environment where people would be comfortable. Their business was one of heart and hard work. Before the first location was built, along with family members, my parents cleared the landscaping and brush where the foundation was poured. They worked hard and accomplished everything they could on their own in order to save money. When the builders came, my parents oversaw everything to ensure the shop was built with quality and care. As they were able to afford and add equipment, they personally transported, hauled, carried and mounted everything they were able to lift.

Ours was truly a family business. Our two-story colonial house stood on the property adjacent to the shop. Each morning during the week, my dad would walk next door allowing himself plenty of time to prep and open the shop, ready to focus on the customers the moment they stepped in the door. My mother answered phones, did bookkeeping and payroll. On the weekends, my father would get on his hands and knees, clean all of the grease stains on the concrete and power wash the building and grounds. My brother, sister and I were responsible for cleaning the shop bathroom and waiting room, and you can bet if it wasn't done properly, we had to do it again. As we got older, my sister and I would help answer phones, greet customers and handle the filing (Ugh! I hated that part). At times, we complained that we would rather be hanging out with friends or watching our favorite television show, but what it taught us was an invaluable work ethic and how to build a successful business.

I vividly remember my father taking the time to walk out from behind his desk (or from under a car) to get to know each customer, well beyond their automotive repair needs. His clients LOVED him, became family friends, and many even delivered gifts at Christmastime. He was referred by colleagues daily because they knew the level of his service would make them shine as well. What my family inherently knew was similar to one of Mickey Mouse's 10 Commandments- Wear Your Guest's Shoes.

An interesting phenomenon happens when people are on the other side of the customer service counter when they are in the position of having to give service as opposed to receiving. Most often the customer concerns are dealt with by following the rules or handling issues the way it's always been done. Businesses tend to forget about the golden rule, about empathy for the customer. We've all heard the excuse, "Sorry that's against policy." We as customers don't really ask for too much. We just want to be taken care of. We want our towels delivered to us rather than having to walk over to the main pool to get them. We want to do business with a company that's going to make our life better.

Most companies are missing the boat with a business model that makes the company run smoothly but is not suitable for the customer's experience. Companies like Nordstrom understand that the customer's experience trumps making life easier for the company.

I know this philosophy firsthand as I worked for Nordstrom for many years. This family-run business stresses the spirit of doing what's right for the customer.

At Nordstrom, I was taught to care for the customer holistical-ly, whether it was warmly greeting them, helping them make the right choices, cheerfully returning things that didn't work out or walking them to another department and introducing them to a sales associate who specialized in what they want-ed. And yes, even picking up a piece of trash thrown on the floor of the dressing room, nothing was off limits because "that isn't my job."

Another retailer (who shall remain nameless) puts their in-ternal processes well before the customer. I made an online purchase that then needed to be returned because the color was not as it appeared on their website. After unsuccessfully attempting the return process online (which was confusing), I called their customer service number. After being on hold for twelve minutes, I was greeted by someone I could not understand. It turned out that the company had outsourced their customer service to another country. While the associate genuinely tried to help me, I was unable to get the answers I needed because of her strong accent. I could not understand her. It may have been good for the company bottom line to outsource their call center, but it was not a good experience for me. I will not buy from them again. Further, I will not refer my clients either. I imagine I'm not the only consumer they've lost.

How can you step into your customer's experience? Begin with their first contact point. It may be their first impression of you personally, or it may be a visit to your website.

Welcome Them

A well-manicured businessman entered an Apple Retail Store, or should I say, stormed into the store. He was having issues with his laptop computer and needed help to resolve the problem. The exchange between the man and the Ap-ple Store greeter began with the gentleman clearly upset and frustrated. Within just a few moments, the Apple associate warmly welcomed him, asked his name, invited him to describe his challenge, acknowledged it and then presented him with a solution that would resolve his issues and concerns in the end. His bad mood instantly shifted from frustration to the assurance of a positive outcome.

On the flip side, a few weeks back my team member Jillian and I were taking a lunch break. We entered a small mom-and-pop health food restaurant where we were the only customers. The regular chef was sitting at one of the tables, texting on her phone. She looked up, saw us and went back to texting. The owner of the restaurant, who glanced up as we walked in, was behind the counter cooking a meal. We walked up to the register and stood for what seemed like five minutes before someone even acknowledged our presence. Turned out, the owner had been cooking a meal for her employee and served that employee before she even spoke to us. Jillian and I were thoroughly annoyed and almost walked out. While we understood that the owner might not have been able to step away from the grill, she could have welcomed us or at least mentioned that she was finishing something up and would be with us shortly. That alone would have made a significant difference.

Whether your customer's first experience of you is live or via your digital presence, a welcome is a crucial first step to developing a relationship that will lead to the ultimate step of hiring you. It may be a warm smile and firm handshake or a welcome video or message on your website. Even a quick email or voicemail that acknowledges them, invites them to learn more or that you are excited about the results your products or services will deliver.

One day when I was working at Nordstrom, a young woman walked into the store wearing ripped jeans (no, not the stylish ones) and a sloppy gray sweatshirt. Her hair was haphazardly thrown up in a ponytail, and she was wearing no makeup. She looked tired and worn out. I quickly greeted her and offered my services, lightly touching her arm in the process. She explained that she was attending a wedding over the weekend and needed a new outfit. Her attitude was less than enthusiastic about the process. She went on to say that she hated shopping but knew that she needed something to wear. "It doesn't need to be amazing, just a dress and shoes." I focused my time and energy on asking questions and learning what she wore that did make her feel confident and attractive. We went on to find a striking jade green dress with matching light bronze sandals, and she even ended up treating herself to a new necklace, earrings, and bracelet ensemble. The finishing touch was an ivory featherweight cashmere pashmina to keep her shoulders warm in the cool, spring evening. Because she mentioned how much she disliked shopping, I walked with her to each department--by her side all the way. I had stepped into her shoes and served her from a place of caring that she would look and feel her best.

The following day I was called in to speak with our store manager. She congratulated me because that customer had written a personal email to the president of Nordstrom explaining that she was touched by the fact that I had not judged her by the way she looked when she entered the store. I had welcomed her. My focus was on learning what was important to her and taking the time to find something that made her feel beautiful. She went on to become one of my most loyal customers, one that ended up spending quite a bit, and often. I was on commission, so that was a plus!! It all started with a warm welcome.

Once that initial welcome has resulted in a business transaction, thank your new client for the honor of working with them and be sure to let them know that you and/or your staff are available to them. I welcome my clients with a hand written card on branded stationary (of course) and send them a small token to brighten their day. (I'll cover a bit more about what you can send your clients in an upcoming section titled "Give a Gift"). Even a successful company like Disney knows it's good practice to acknowledge an individual's initial business transaction. When vacationers book a Disney trip, they receive a welcome package in the mail. The box is full of items (like short videos) to get the travelers excited and educated about their trip. Think of ways to welcome your customers that will connect them to the experience they will have with you.

Clear Communication

Whether you are in a service-based business or provide your customers with tangible products, it's important to clearly communicate what they can expect from you. This is yet another opportunity to step into your customer's shoes. Create a step-by-step description of the process/timeline you use, and then send this to your new client. They'll know what to expect, and it's a useful touchpoint for them to experience a positive connection with you. Be sure to let them know that their experience matters and that they should feel free to reach out if they have any questions. Then, be quick in your responses.

My team and I have a process for connecting with our clients when they purchase one of our programs. Once a client signed up for my most recent webinar, we sent step-by-step guidelines for how to prepare and get the most out of it. First, we stressed that they should calendar all of the webinar dates and take note of the call-in details right on their calendar entry, so they weren't frantically looking for them at the last minute. We also encouraged them to be on the webinar live so they could participate in the Q&A and take advantage of some bonuses we were only offering to those attendees on the live webinar.

Next we addressed the setting where they would hear the webinar and urged them to create an environment that would allow them to focus without distractions. In other words, a quiet space where they could maximize the investment they had made in the program. One of the preparations I undertake in my own home is arranging my family's schedule and meals to minimize possible interruptions. I take that a step further, close my office door and post a note that reads, "It can wait. No really, it can wait!" Finally, we ended each communication to our webinar clients with an invitation to email us directly with any questions they might have. As clients transition into my VIP programs, they have my personal cell phone number and are welcome to call or text me.

Communicating and delivering your processes smoothly is an absolute must in creating an ideal customer experience. Whether it's the technology you utilize in scheduling and confirming client appointments or following up with the personal contacts you make, be certain to deliver your services in an organized and concise manner. The purchasing process should be quick and smooth; and if you are shipping, do so promptly and provide for a simple return process.

Over Deliver

Tony Hsieh, CEO of Zappos, has built a brand noted for its excellent customer service. Clearly it has been a success! As an avid online shopper, I consistently patronize companies that give great service. So when a new pair of Gucci flats arrives but pinch my heel, I have no worries about a seamless return with Zappos. Giving more than what is expected is always a nice touch. If your client is expecting a 45-minute consult with you, plan to give them a bit more by design. This is an opportunity to read your customer and ascertain whether to extend your time or stick to your initial time agreement. You might say something like, "Our session time is coming to a close, but I recognize we need a little longer. I want to be sure you feel complete." It's not necessary to do it every time, but a little extra every once in a while lets your clients know that you operate from a serve-first mindset, and that's great for brand identity.

Over delivering may be in the form of allowing yourself ample time to complete a client project and then delivering early, thereby beating the deadline. One of the photographers I use promises to provide her images within a week and often delivers them to my clients and me within just a few days. It's a pleasant and memorable surprise.

On a recent visit to Bellagio on Lake Como, my husband and I stopped in a small boutique that sold scarves. It was the first of many shopping excursions on our trek to the Mediterranean. Inside the shop, we were surrounded by an array of beautiful colors, fabrics, and fine weaves. We thoughtfully made our selections—gifts for friends and family. When it came time to make our purchases the owner of the shop (who by the way was the matriarch of the family-owned business) carefully folded and wrapped each scarf in gold tissue secured by a bronze sticker, then placed them in the shop's branded box that she tied with a silk ribbon. She knew that treating our purchases with care and wrapping them like precious gifts would heighten our experience, and we would treasure the choices we made. Also, the friends and family members we bought for were absolutely thrilled, too!!

Another way to over deliver is to thoughtfully remember your clients and customers on their special days- be it a birthday or during the holiday season. Even a hand-written note (just because) is a powerful way to convey that you care. As I build relationships with my clients, I am listening with an ear for those special days that have meaning to them. Do they have an anniversary coming up? Is their significant other having a major surgery? I will literally ask the date and then make note of it in my calendar. It might be a text message or voicemail the day of their husband's surgery to let them know I'm thinking of them.

One technique I use to deliver value to my clients is using my network to benefit them. They are pleased to find the celebration of their accomplishments front and center on my social media platform complete with a link to promote a program they've launched, a new television interview or book.

The personal brand and image progression of my VIP clients (as long as they've consented) is openly celebrated on my social media platform. I do this for the trusted experts I've hired to create the deliverables as well. This consistently results in bringing awareness to the birth of their up level and attracts new customers!

Give more by asking your clients what else they need. Routinely, ask them how you could go further, provide better service, and be more useful to them. They will almost always be delighted that you asked. More importantly, their answers should provide valuable information, and their requests will generally cost you little or nothing to deliver. Your efforts will be appreciated.

Give A Gift

As my business evolved, I began receiving designer clothing that would just show up at my door, and those days I felt like a kid on Christmas morning, complete with flying tissue paper. When a package shows up on my front doorstep, I can't wait to see what's inside! My husband thinks I act like a little kid, and he is absolutely right. When I receive a surprise gift, the thoughtfulness makes me feel loved, and the enclosed trinket is a huge bonus. No doubt you know exactly what it's like to receive a thoughtful gift and what a difference it can make in your day.

Sending a surprise is one of my favorite customer experience touchpoints because I LOVE receiving little niceties (hint, hint :)) and know my clients do as well. Giving gifts is a great way to spoil your customers and make them feel like royalty. Send a beautifully branded, hand-written note card just because and include a gift card for a coffee or a personally branded token. For example, I send a sparkling ballpoint pen with a stylus in a black velvet pouch or a sleek sewing kit for on-the-go, each of these branded.

If you are a product-based business, include a little extra when you ship your product. My clients receive their products in a beautiful silver padded envelope and are always delighted to find something special inside. Rent The Runway is brilliant at executing this concept. Not only am I in complete anticipation of wearing a beautiful designer gown to my special event, but they always take it a step further. When I receive my dress, it comes in a branded zippered garment bag and tucked inside is a small pouch with oodles of product samples from major name brands.

Not sure what to give? Think about small tokens you've received in the past. Things that made you feel special and spoiled or something useful or innovative that you never knew you needed until you opened the package. Another way to come up with great items is to connect with colleagues who have product samples they would like to highlight and promote. It can be a real win-win! You can also reach out to your promotional products expert to find just the right thing for your customers. My go-to expert is Robin Richter, President of Wearable Imaging, Inc. http://www.wearableimaging.com. Her company specializes in quality promotional products. I get my branded sparkle pens and other goodies from her.

Problem Solving

Discover, Acknowledge, Respond

You may have heard that there are no problems in business, only opportunities to create great customer solutions. The very first step in problem solving is to discover your customer's needs and acknowledge them. Apple sets a terrific benchmark for acknowledgement of their customer's problem. Not long ago I visited an Apple Retail Store and was searching for a clicker that would advance my presentation screens on my laptop. The apparently new sales associate said they didn't have exactly what I was looking for. I was surprised by her answer and asked to speak to the store manager. The sales manager, Jim, took the time to really listen to my feedback about why this item is a must for what I'm sure is a core segment of their target market. He smiled, nodded and then said, "I know this device you're looking for is important to you, and I really do wish I had a solution to offer. Let's explore your needs a little further." He then went on to ask some questions and ascertain if one of their other options might work. He took notes and promised to make my feedback known at the corporate level. Jim was not able to offer an immediate solution, but simply by listening and acknowledging my desires I was a happy customer. We went on to talk about Apple's customer service philosophies, and in the end, I asked if we could get a picture together, one that I ended up posting on my social platforms, praising Apple for their service!

Once the 'problem' has been discovered and acknowledged, it is time to respond. Notice that this step is respond--not react. A thoughtful response (not a defensive one) is what is called for when addressing customer concerns. It's imperative not to take complaints personally but look at them as an opportunity to improve future customer interactions. A thoughtful response might be offering a quick solution or may even be more conversation about what your client sees as the solution. Asking for her input is yet another opportunity to listen to and acknowledge her. Moreover, it is through that inquiry you will learn what solutions are important to your clients and will undoubtedly improve your overall customer experience.

Once you've responded to the 'problem', you can then address the internal quality control process, which will avoid repeats of the same issue. It will ensure that your processes will improve. More than for your existing customers, this internal improvement will allow you to gain new customers or even widen the scope of your product/service base.

The final step is to thank the client for taking the time to voice her opinion and offer valuable feedback. These customers are 'gold' because they're the ones who provided you with an opportunity to shine, rather than walk out the door and complain to all of their friends. Each industry varies in the multiple possible solutions offered, but it's important to keep in mind that the rare customer or client may never be fully satisfied. In such cases, it may ultimately be best to offer a return or refund for services not yet rendered.

Discovering, Acknowledging and Responding are a surefire way to make your customers feel heard and will provide valuable opportunities to set your own platinum standard of service!

Keep In Touch

It is six to seven times more costly to attract a new customer than it is to retain an existing customer. Keeping in touch with your clients once your initial business transaction is complete lets them know they are more than just a paycheck, and they really matter to you. Your professional relationship with them continues as long as you are in business.

Five years ago I hired a business coach who taught me some very valuable lessons mostly by what she did right, but also through some of the missteps she made in her customer service. One of the things that really struck me about her was once our coaching sessions were completed, I was unable to get even a return email or phone call when I had a quick question relevant to a program we had designed together. To be clear, the message I received by her non-response was, "You're no longer writing me a check, so don't bother me." Had she taken even a few minutes to respond to my emails or the voicemail I left, I would have been much more likely to refer business to her. In her shortsightedness, she lost referrals I would have made.

There are numerous ways to continue the relationship like sending your clients resources you know will enhance their personal brand. It can be as simple as a link to a blog post about their field of expertise or sharing one of their insightful posts on your social media platform. Keeping in touch may be remembering them on their birthday with a simple, yet thoughtful gift. My favorite is a spontaneous phone call to say hello and ask how they're doing with no agenda other than to check in. With digital overload, a quick call will stand out and make your customer feel cared for.

By developing the ever-important Customer Experience, you establish trust and create relationships, so your customers will want to repurchase your products or services. Additionally, when your customers are happy, they become promoters and attract new customers to your business—that's the $10,000 in free advertising.

Chapter Seven

Conclusion

-7-

Conclusion

We've covered the 5 Keys to a Profitable Personal Brand in detail. You've learned the power and simplicity of creating a brand identity simply by being the best version of who you are. No doubt you've taken a look in the mirror or your closet to determine if your visual voice is reflecting the image you want to grow. You may have a mini-me sitting on your shoulder whispering, "sit up straight" or "enter the room with confidence and a smile." You've probably taken a quick inventory of your online presence and made some minor (if not major) tweaks. Quite possibly you've sent a request to your clients for feedback on the experience they've had with you.

Each of these elements is proven to make an impact, but the most important factor is the renewed confidence in how you perceive yourself. You are challenging those old negative messages: Who do you think you are? You can never do this. Stop attracting so much attention or stop hiding in the corner. You're just another pretty face or you aren't pretty enough. You see the profound meaning of the work you do and how elevating the way you see yourself, in turn, benefits those around you.

Your Personal Brand Dream Team

Cultivating a solid and compelling personal brand and image takes a team of experienced professionals who creatively and professionally collaborate to reflect the success of who you are so you'll attract your ideal clients and compel them to act. Over the years, I've worked with various professionals who have helped me to hone my business and brand. The expertise in their given field has elevated my business in ways I could not have managed solo. Elevate your brand persona and step into action as you consider your dream team.

Personal Brand Coach
Image Coach
Marketing Expert
Health Coach
Hair Stylist
Makeup Artist
Photographer
Graphic Designer
Web Designer
Video Production Team
Live or Virtual Assistant

You may have coaches or experts who are a combination of two or three of the above but beware of hiring someone who thinks they can do it all themselves. Ask yourself, has this person chosen their area of expertise, really?

Pinpointing who to use can be a challenge. It's essential to vet carefully the professionals you choose. Begin with one (from the list above) that you trust implicitly; then ask for referrals to experts they have worked with personally or have consistently referred clients--clients who were very happy with their results. Peruse their work to ensure it has a look and feel that resonates with you. Then ask to speak with at least two of their existing clients so you can ask the questions important to you. My favorite questions are: What do you love about the work (s)he has done for you? Is there one thing you think needs improvement in their process or end product?

In Closing

Close your eyes for a moment (well, after you've read this paragraph). Step back into your childhood when you still believed in the Tooth Fairy and Santa Claus. What did you dream of becoming? Was it a compassionate nurse who saved lives? A brave astronaut who stepped on to the moon? An advocate for the endangered animals on our earth? Did you believe you could fly if you jumped from your treehouse? Did you know, without a doubt, that you could change lives and make an imprint? Did you feel pretty? Did you strut your stuff and smile at yourself in the mirror when you played 'dress up'?

I hope by now you understand the secret sauce of a successful brand persona is owning those childhood dreams and your ultimate potential as a woman and professional, stepping beyond your past hurts, not letting them define who you are, but understanding they have refined the beautiful woman you've become. My wish is that *The Total Package* has and will continue to inspire, challenge and free you to develop your own unique and profitable total package.

About the Author
JuliAnn Stitick

For the last 20 years, JuliAnn Stitick has helped powerful, successful people align their personal brand with their ultimate potential and accelerate their business success. Whether working privately with her clients or leading a keynote for a business conference, JuliAnn's sincere and strategic approach compels game-changing insights and actions that ultimately transform lives and paychecks. JuliAnn is a trusted advisor for top level entrepreneurs globally, Oscar and Golden Globe Winners and organizations crossing every industry—Lexus, Disney, Nordstrom, Kaiser Permanente, Caruso Affiliated and Los Angeles Women Police Officers & Associates. She does what she loves—developing the very best in each client.

JuliAnn also volunteers her time and expertise through her involvement with The Salvation Army, Girl Scouts of America, The eWomenNetwork Foundation and youth groups. She works in close collaboration with these dynamic organizations, building strong leadership teams and facilitating fundraising efforts. But most of all, JuliAnn enjoys the opportunity to mentor young women before they enter the workforce.

JuliAnn is married to Joe; together they live in the quiet suburban foothills north of Los Angeles, California, with their son, Alec, and two lovable dogs Tanner and Wolfie. A mother of three and grandmother of one, JuliAnn spends her leisure time with her family, camping, traveling, bbq'ing, reading and watching movies.

Connect with JuliAnn Stitick

Website: www.JuliAnnStitick.com
Email: support@JuliAnnStitick.com

LinkedIn: www.LinkedIn.com/in/JuliAnnStitick
Facebook: www.facebook.com/YourSuccessStyle/
Twitter: www.Twitter.com/JuliAnnStitick
Instagram: www.Instagram.com/JuliAnnStitick/
YouTube: JuliAnn Stitick- http://bit.ly/1QdvUFl
Pinterest: www.Pinterest.com/JuliAnnStitick/
Mailing Address: 601 East Glenoaks Boulevard, Suite 206,
                    Glendale, CA 91207

I'm So Grateful to You...

I have tears in my eyes and my heart swells as I thank you from the bottom of my heart for spending your precious time with me while you read this book. When you implement the lessons you've learned, you'll begin to see yourself in a new way- more beautiful than ever and confidently ready to reveal the best of you to the world.

This book is an expression of my passion, mission and vision that all women have the ability to see themselves from a place of love, value, and worth. If you are willing to pass this message on, I'd greatly appreciate you telling your friends and sharing what you loved about this book by providing a review on my Amazon sales page.

Thanks a bunch!

Acknowledgements

I am deeply grateful to the precious people in my life - encouraging me to spread my wings and fly.

Thank you to my husband Joe, for wholeheartedly supporting my journey all the way and never once questioning my dreams and vision. I'm so glad we found each other.

Thank you to my kids Perrin, Amanda and Alec. I love each of you dearly and thank you for the life lessons you have so wisely taught me.

Thank you to my parents Dick and Judy, for the incredible life you've provided. The gift of your example has been the foundation of my life. I love you so much.

To my brother Gary, for sharing laughter and tears and tears because of laughter. To my sister Janine, for a journey of love and support.

Thank you to my support system- Jillian, for being my right hand, left hand and everything in between. You are a treasure. To Lisa, for always being my champion and lovingly pushing me to stretch beyond what I think is possible. To Starla, for beautifully capturing the essence of who I am. To Becky, for your exquisite designs. To Steve and Jaime, for your creative genius and vision. To Robbin for your patient guidance. To Mom and Sarah for lending your eye for detail in the final book edits.

To my closest friends Eileen, Lisa, Mary Ann, Luz, Mary and Holly for your unwavering friendship through the good times and the bad times.

You all truly bless me!

References

Brooks, Rechele, and Andrew N. Meltzoff. "The Importance of Eyes: How Infants Interpret Adult Looking Behavior." Developmental Psychology 38.6 (2002): 958 - 966. PMC. Web. 29 Dec. 2015

Corcoran, Barbara, "About": http://www.BarbaraCorcoran.com/about, 2015

If You Don't Have Big Breasts, Put Ribbons on Your Pigtails: And Other Lessons I Learned from My Mom, 2003 http://www.barbaracorcoran.com/pigtails/, 2015

Cuddy, A. J. C. Presence: Bringing Your Boldest Self to Your Biggest Challenges. Little, Brown, & Co: New York, NY. 2015

Gallup Strengths Center, Strengths Finder 2.0 Assessment, https://www.gallupstrengthscenter.com, Copyright 2014 Gallup, Inc.

Hogshead, Sally. The Fascination Advantage Assessment, http://www.howtofascinate.com/, Copyright 2015 Fascinate, Inc.

Mehrabian, Dr. Albert: Professor Emeritus of Psychology at UCLA, https://www.psych.ucla.edu/faculty/page/mehrab, 2015.

Perfect Sense Digital with Patrick McClenahan, "LA2015: Creating the Logo" video: http://www.la2015.org/videos/la2015-the-logo, 2015

Petry Leanse, Ellen, "Just" Say No: https://www.linkedin.com/pulse/just-say-ellen-petry-leanse , May 29, 2015

Made in the USA
San Bernardino, CA
15 January 2016